WINDY CITY STORIES

JAMES DOHREN

BROWN POSEY PRESS

an imprint of Sunbury Press, Inc.
Mechanicsburg, PA USA

an imprint of Sunbury Press, Inc.
Mechanicsburg, PA USA

For information about special discounts for bulk purchases, please contact Sunbury Press Orders Dept. at (855) 338-8359 or orders@sunburypress.com.

To request one of our authors for speaking engagements or book signings, please contact Sunbury Press Publicity Dept. at publicity@sunburypress.com.

ISBN: 978-1-62006-337-8 (Trade Paperback)

Library of Congress Control Number: 2019950577

FIRST BROWN POSEY PRESS EDITION: October 2019

Product of the United States of America
0 1 1 2 3 5 8 13 21 34 55

Set in Adobe Garamond
Designed by Crystal Devine
Cover by Terry Kennedy
Edited by Erika Hodges

Continue the Enlightenment!

CONTENTS

FOREWORD

Windy City Stories began with a series of e-mails between myself and Lawrence Knorr, publisher of Sunbury Press. Sunbury Press had published an earlier book I'd written, *Letters from a Shoebox*. That book was based on a cache of Civil War letters from young men and women from rural Ohio who wrote to each other from 1862-1865. I attempted to interpret and describe the lives of each of the half-dozen letter writers. I enjoyed writing that book because through many readings of the letters and exhaustive research I came to be intimately bound up in their lives.

After a time, Lawrence e-mailed me to ask if I had done any other non-fiction writing and, as it turned out, I had. These pieces though written in a more casual, informal style were equally well-researched. I sent several of them to Lawrence. Because I lived and worked near the city of Chicago some of the stories were Chicago related. Lawrence suggested a book of stories about Chicago, and he agreed when I asked if I could choose my own topics. I asked him how many stories or chapters he wanted. The suggested number of twenty was high enough that it caused me to back away from the project for a time.

Then, as they say, fate entered the picture. Or, to be more precise, health came along in just about the worst sense of the word. Two of my heart valves failed at the same time and I had to have open-heart surgery immediately to replace one and have the other repaired. There was a serious complication. Instead of being on a heart-lung machine for two hours I was attached for five and it didn't help that I was a seventy-something. I had a very slow recovery, spending twenty-three days in the ICU partly due to other complications, then another seven days in observation. However, thanks to the collective skills of my surgical team, many other doctors and nurses, and tremendous support from my family and friends, I obviously survived.

Yes, I was alive but I was still in pretty awful condition when I got back home. Without the unfailing and exhaustive help of my wife, I would have been confined to a rehabilitation unit somewhere. I consider my survival a miracle, really. I had a lot of recovering to do and it would take almost two years to accomplish. While I wasn't exactly a shut-in, most of my outings were trips to doctors and labs. However, I hadn't forgotten Lawrence's book proposal. Without exaggeration, it became a priceless restorative therapy for me, mentally, physically, and emotionally.

The many hours under anesthesia had left me with terrible tremors in both hands. It was even hard for me to eat with utensils and I couldn't write or type without great concentration and persistence. I spent a lot of time being furious at my helplessness and loss of control. Outdoor activities were impossible and I could easily surf through 80+ cable channels and not find anything I thought worthwhile. I loved to read, but I could manage only a ten to fifteen-minute attention span.

That's why this new proposal was such a God-send. Visiting nurses came, did their best, and left, but nothing they did could relieve my boredom or frustration. Challenging myself with the struggle to create new story ideas, gather research notes, organize them into outline form, then begin writing draft after draft was the best therapy possible, I believe. Thank God for the internet.

I am not a patient person by nature, but now instead of frustration and depression I found the absorption in the writing process was keeping me calm. There were times when I lost my temper, ripped off a string of curses and pounded my computer desk, but somehow managing to avoid smashing my keyboard. Everything that used to be easy was now difficult. It was taking me ten times longer to do the same things I did so easily before. My fingers seemed to delight in dragging over keys I didn't mean to hit. Sometimes I had to recreate whole paragraphs of hand-written material I couldn't read. On nights when sleep didn't come, I would open a story file and work until two or three in the morning. Then I'd eat breakfast and go back to sleep for a few hours.

As the months passed, my tremors gradually eased through my writing therapy but have not yet totally disappeared. I am resolved that they will always be there to some extent. It's hard now to remember how many of my typing mistakes are reminders of my disability and how many would have happened without it. My handwriting remains cramped and barely legible, but at least I can regularly read it.

All along I was finding pleasure in discovering new story ideas that I thought others would enjoy and writing them in my own particular style. Some were more personal, but some were also about subjects Chicagoans might be familiar with but not those unfamiliar with the city. There are a few that might not be known by those who have lived in the great city by the lake all their lives.

I wanted to avoid stories which were clichés or otherwise too commonly known, so in this book, you will find no story about the Great Fire of 1871, none about any of the events represented by the stars on Chicago's flag, none about the Bears, Bulls, Black Hawks, White Sox, or, despite the temptation, even about the Cubs.

I had lots of other inspiration for my recovery including my family and all my friends. There were other activities which helped me focus on recovery so I can never know with certainty what course my recovery would have taken without the work on this new book, but I think I am safe in saying it would have been slower, more miserable, and possibly might not have happened at all.

1

"THE 77"

CHICAGO'S NEIGHBORHOODS

Every city has its beginning and Chicago is no exception. It began as a fragile community built on ground barely above water level in the dismal, malarial swamps and sloughs that surrounded it and at the southern end of Lake Michigan. The name "Chicago" came from the Indian word for the wild onions whose fragrance permeated the air. It was Indian territory, a trading post for the French, Native American, and American trappers and traders who formed the tiny community huddled around the meager protection of the now long-gone Ft. Dearborn.

As with all cities, Chicago has constantly needed stimulus to grow. There is a possibly apocryphal story that a group of hopeful bankers and business leaders from Chicago trekked to the then capital of Illinois, Vandalia, to ask for loans for investment. Their reception was cold, to say the least. It was made pretty clear that they were considered country bumpkins by the good citizens they appealed to. They were told that they'd barely heard of this "Chicago" and it was too far from the Ohio and Mississippi Rivers to ever amount to much. Obviously, the loan request was denied as too risky.

As it nearly always can, technology came to scramble things up. The Erie Canal was completed in 1825 and quickly turned the Great Lakes into inland seas with dozens of safe harbors and increasing business based on the transportation of lumber, cheap Midwestern grains, and

1

farm produce east. In 1848, the Illinois-Michigan Canal was completed, connecting the Great Lakes with the Mississippi River and the Gulf of Mexico with Chicago as its nexus of trade. There were no longer falls, rapids, or shallows that required multiple transfers of goods and passengers.

Railroads shook off their perilous beginnings and followed commerce. If there were great forests, they made good material for track ties. If there were wetlands to fill and drain west of the Appalachians, there were no mountain grades to engineer, rock to blast or canyons to span. With ever-increasing competition, speed, safety, and efficiency, they drove down costs and difficulty of cross-country commerce.

As the railroads waxed, the canals waned. They were just too slow, complex, and expensive to build and maintain. Railroads spread like a web across the landscape eventually connecting nearly all towns large and small to one another. With a strategic position on Lake Michigan, Chicago was the logical place to transfer goods and passengers from eastern trains to those headed farther west. Chicago prospered. It all happened so abruptly and quickly it gave those rebuffed Chicago investors some good time to toast each other and gloat over their promotion from "country bumpkin" to "city slicker."

Easy and cheap transportation brought a flood of workers to labor in the steel mills, on the railroads, at the stockyards and packing houses, and in the construction of a booming city. The work was simple and easy to learn, but brutal. All it took was blood, sweat, determination, and learning never to complain or question. Chicago truly was the "City of Big Shoulders" that Carl Sandburg recognized.

America has always been built by immigrants fleeing poverty and oppression in the Old Country and Chicago was the perfect place for immigrants to settle into a new life. They usually began their American life in an enclave or ghetto of those who came from the same regions they left. Here they could feel comfortable with their own churches, schools, newspapers, theaters, festivals, and other customs. Some of Chicago's oldest neighborhoods began as immigrant settlements. The Irish, Italians, Polish, Germans, Czechs, Swedes, and the Dutch all came and brought a different culture to each neighborhood. At one time or another you could visit Andersonville (Swedish), Posen (Polish), and Pilsen (Czech) communities. I'll let the reader decide the original ethnic identities of Ukrainian Village, Greektown, Little Italy, and Chinatown. A person could live an entire lifetime and never have to learn a word of English expect perhaps for work. Or, more likely to give a better chance for assimilation, the goal of nearly all the second and third generations of immigrant families. Assimilation assumed moving away from the old neighborhood to one where they could shed the stigma and prejudice of being "foreign."

As one ethnic group gradually left, another took its place. Presently these old neighborhoods might be occupied by residents from Mexico or Latin American nations, Puerto Rico and many Caribbean countries, and thousands from the Indian subcontinent and Southeast Asia. During the Great Migration thousands of Blacks fleeing the Jim Crow South came to Chicago on the many railroads.

When new generations did achieve acceptance into general society they also prospered in wealth. They now had enough resources to move to one of the new middle-class developments being built for those who could afford to leave the mud, dust, stink, noise, and dangers of the city. Not quite suburbs but close. These areas gave them a chance to have an apartment or, the dream of all, a home of their own. Untold numbers of the famous Chicago Bungalows were built as sturdy and roomy homes for the upward bound.

The new prosperity also created great wealth for some from commerce, industry, agriculture, finance, and, ironically, land development. Retail giants Sears and Roebuck and Montgomery Ward both called Chicago home. Mansions that covered entire blocks were built in Hyde Park in or near the University of Chicago campus. More could be found in the close-in Prairie District and Gold Coast.

Developers recognized a trend when they saw one and cashed in by buying up vast swaths of cheap and vacant prairie land to convert into small islands of new homes. They plotted and planned, then prepared the land by paving roads with brick, installing sewer and water lines, and

A Chicago bungalow.

gas for lighting. Soon electricity made its way into homes to power an ever-growing host of electric appliances to make life easier and to keep the economy humming. Sloughs and swamps were drained or reconfigured into parks with small lakes for boating, fishing, or family gatherings.

As the population spread so did the transportation net. First horse or mule-drawn streetcars, then electric powered street cars and interurban light rail lines grew in number and length. This convenient and cheap transportation allowed workers to arrive at work promptly, clean and dry.

While the land was developed the new areas come to be called "sides," North Side, West Side, and South Side. No East Side unless you were a fish. From Rogers Park and Lincoln Square on the North, to Humboldt and Garfield Parks on the West Side, Pullman, and Hegeweich on the South Side they grew. At the center of it all was the Loop, so named for the circle of elevated railroad or "El" that encircled it. Inside the Loop were the most important businesses and exclusive retail stores.

Probably the best known of these planned communities was George Pullman's company town modestly named Pullman. Sturdy brick row houses for families, apartments for singles, and detached homes for executives rose. Employees and their families were required to live in company housing and do all their shopping in the company stores, go to the company provided houses of worship, infirmary, and become involved in company activities. Naturally, for a people with restless feet and determined habits, there was some cheating, particularly about following Pullman's strict prohibition rules. The model worked as long as the Pullman Palace Co. continued to grow and wages along with it.

In the mid-1890s it all come to a violent, tragic end as a combination of competition and saturation of the sleeping car market caused sales to slump. Repair and refurbishing of the cars weren't enough to keep the company afloat. In addition, the Panic of 1893 dried up any financing Pullman could have normally expected. The result was that wages were reduced but not the cost of goods and services. Workers were soon living on starvation incomes and enraged to learn that full dividends were being paid to shareholders and directors. Anyone who dared complain was evicted from their home and fired. The United Railroad Workers (URW) union which Pullman despised stepped in to organize the workers in 1894 and a strike was soon called. Emotions became explosive until a deadly riot occurred at Pullman. Union leaders received prison sentences and the union was "busted." In a fitting end of its own, the Pullman Co. never recovered. In 1898, only four years after the bloody riot, Pullman's once proud company was ordered into bankruptcy by the courts. The town dwindled and much of it was abandoned.

But the story of Pullman was far from over. As the city neighborhoods filled in and property and living costs increased, younger generations discovered Pullman only twelve miles from the Loop and a stop on the Chicago and South Shore (electric) Railroad. The sturdy buildings were run-down after many years of neglect but their bones were good. Even considering restoration costs the homes and flats were cheap enough to afford with most of the original hardwood and other decorative features in good condition inside and the handsome brick architecture outside. It helped a great deal that much of it had been originally designed as housing. Pullman soon became the newest place to be.

Pullman was re-invented and its story is an example, but it was far from being the first or only neighborhood to do so. Each of the 77 neighborhoods has undergone the process at least once. By the mid-twentieth century, the fully-built city was being carefully examined for new chances for neighborhood improvement or "gentrification." Every sound, empty warehouse or defunct factory was a possible loft building. Every old apartment building became a possibility for conversion to luxury condominiums. New money and new life were pumped into the neighborhoods. However, it wasn't good for everyone as long-term residents were once again forced out by rising property values and costs of living.

One neighborhood feature which rarely changed with the population and lifestyle was the name. Let's take an imaginary tour of a few of the 77 to learn how they got those names. Most were chosen by the developers to give a touch of class but a few got a nickname based on their history. They range from the most humble and obvious to the grand. Ashtown, for instance, got its nickname because it was a popular place for people to dump their furnace ashes. Bucktown was named for the goats raised there by Polish immigrants. Back of the Yards was the neighborhood surrounding the once thriving stockyards which employed thousands of residents. On the other end of the spectrum are the Gold Coast and Magnificent Mile or even little Avalon Park. Andersonville was an area settled by Swedes after the Chicago Fire of 1871. Old Town was just as it says, but was once known as "cabbage town" for the truck farms that occupied the land. Bronzeville got its name from a theater critic for the African-American newspaper, *Chicago Bee* for the skin color of its residents. Bronzeville became a backdrop for the celebrated Black Renaissance of the '30s and '40s mostly in the arts. Edison Park was named to honor the great inventor decades before his death. Garfield and McKinley Parks were named for martyred presidents. Douglas Park for one of the participants in the Lincoln-Douglas debates and Lincoln Park and Lincoln Square for the other. No surprise then that there is a Washington Park and Jefferson Park. Some got their names because of some prominent geographic feature such as Chicago Ridge, Stony Island, Edgewater, Lakeview, Fernwood, and Rosedale.

There are also neighborhoods named for once prominent people who are now largely unknown. These include Humboldt Park (Humboldt was a nineteenth-century naturalist and explorer) and, rather strangely, Gladstone Park, for the four-time Prime Minister of Britain. Logan Square is for John A. Logan, a heroic Civil War general and U.S. Senator from Illinois. Bridgeport was once the town at the northern end of the Illinois-Michigan Canal It is still the family seat of both Mayors Daley. Sauganash is a land of sloughs, small shallow lakes, and forest preserves. Despite the city's name and its beginning in Indian territory, only Sauganash is named for a Native American. The origin of Wrigleyville is simple. On the South Side, the White Sox play in good old Bridgeport.

Every neighborhood had smaller areas which have instilled fierce loyalty in its residents. It has always been that ex-Chicagoans identify themselves by their neighborhood. Get them talking and they will instantly mention the schools, church, or intersection that defined where they grew up. The city eventually expanded to annex them all into the great metropolitan area of Chicago.

Wrigley Field. (Courtesy of Rdikeman at the English Wikipedia.)

To recognize the seamless metropolitan city of today with its millions of residents, it helps to have an analogy. There are a few. Maybe a volcano with lava flowing over everything; but no, the spread of Chicago was neither deadly or fiery. Well, except for 1871, that is. There's a glacier too. Relentless it may be but also still very slow and cold. I even thought about an aspen clone which spreads over everything and is at least a living organism, but, no, that's not good enough. Finally, I thought about a family which begins small, just a few people living together but growing over generations to absorb people of all character, color, temperament, and culture into its fold. Think of Chicago's growth to absorb all villages and squares, parks, ridges, and heights and yet allow each to maintain its original character and architecture to change for better or worse, to be good or evil and yet still be part of this great city. Then you will better understand Chicago's neighborhoods.

2

GETTING AROUND TOWN

CHICAGO'S STREET RAILROADS

We think nothing of hopping into one of our cars and driving five or more miles to shop, dine, or find entertainment. We're willing to commute long distances to work every day so we can live in a neighborhood we enjoy. It's quick and easy unless the traffic is snarled and then the drive will be long and tiresome. Traffic or no traffic it's still clean, comfortable, and increasingly safe.

As you know, it wasn't always that way. The dominance of auto travel is a relatively recent phenomenon, rising only in the 1950s. In the days when autos were just one more expensive way to display wealth, only the wealthy had them. All the better that they came with another servant, the chauffeur/mechanic.

The 99 percent had to find other solutions to get around town. At first, they walked to shops they needed. Every few blocks would be a mom and pop convenience store with food staples being the main inventory. In the days when the only refrigeration was an ice box, the housewife would have to make several trips a week to bring home the small amounts that could be safely stored. Corner groceries were convenient and closer to home but their goods were both more limited and more expensive. When she had time, the wife and mother might have had time to stop by local specialty shops such as the butcher, the baker, and I would be surprised if there wasn't a shop selling candle sticks. At these specialty shops she would find a wider selection at lower prices. While walking was good exercise, it was not seen as enjoyable by a hard-working homemaker. It would be much nastier and more dangerous in bad weather. Workers also had to get to their jobs and children to school. While the streets were always safe, it was still a long walk there and back and Mom couldn't come to pick you up in bad weather.

At first, horse-drawn travel was an unreachable luxury for most families. It meant the expense of keeping a horse, a stable and carriage house, and so forth. Stage coaches were also expensive and didn't cover much of the city. Why not bring the advantages of horse-drawn travel to the masses by having horses pull cars on rails? Many passengers each paying a reasonable fare might prove profitable. And the lines were relatively cheap to build. It was a good enough idea to garner what we would now call "venture capital." Permits were secured to run the rails on city streets. Money was also needed for livestock and rolling stock and to pay employees. Chicago's first horse car railway began service back in 1859. The cars carried up to ten passengers and required one or two horses. Almost as soon as horse-drawn railroads began, the disadvantages started to appear. While they did make it possible to allow riders to escape walking in the filth of paved and unpaved streets or being run over by a freight wagon, it was barely faster, maybe even slower than walking. Horses were a problem. First there was only so much one or two horsepower could pull. The horse teams could only work a few hours a day. Chicago City Railways (CCRY) had to bear the expense of 6,000 horses and the attendant feed, water, grooms, stables and stable hands, harnesses, and horse doctors. It wasn't unusual for a horse to die in harness and snarl traffic, effectively wrecking the schedule until the corpse could be hauled away. Thousands of horses died in the Chicago Fire and then, a year after, equine epizootic. If that wasn't enough, fares could not be raised because the state legislature had permanently capped a fare at five cents, a reasonable fare at the time but eventually ruinous.

A new system was sorely needed. At first small steam locomotives were used but constant complaints from citizens about noise, soot, and sparks caused the CCRY to abandon them. Investors cast their eyes westward to San Francisco's cable cars and brought the technology to Chicago. Large power houses were built at various points in the city. Each contained massive furnaces to create steam to turn turbines which powered large winding machines attached to miles of cable. The miles of cable were buried in a shallow trench between the tracks. Hundreds of new cars were ordered, both open for summer and closed for winter. Given Chicago's climate, the open cars were soon abandoned. Each car was operated by a team of motorman and a conductor. The motorman had a cable grip lever which he could release to let the car stop and re-engage to start up again. He was also equipped with a loud bell to signal stops and departures and warn away pedestrians. The conductor was charged with collecting fares and keeping track of passengers to prevent free-loaders from hopping on. The capacity for carrying passengers greatly increased. The system was so reliable that eighty miles of track were laid between 1890 to 1906. Despite all the start-up costs, the cable railways had brought down the per mile cost. By that latter date all horse-drawn service ended within the city.

At about the same time, the first successful electric-powered street car was introduced. The advantages over the cable system were obvious. The electric cars could carry more passengers for less money and installation was cheaper and faster. And in a climate like Chicago's, the cable trench could easily take in melting snow and freeze.

By that time and until the end of the street car era, no matter the manufacturer or size, wooden or steel, all street cars had the same design. Doors at the front for entrance and doors at the center or back for exiting. All cars were enclosed and nearly all had screens for warm weather and storm windows for cold. Windows could be raised for ventilation, but putting a hand or head out the window was impossible. There were heaters for cold weather but no air conditioning,

All cars had a cowcatcher to prevent pedestrians from being dragged under the car. The wheel "trucks" could swivel to make sharper turning easier. On more crowded routes and during rush hours cars would be coupled to form a train. There were specialty cars too. Since good track traction was vital, there were cars fitted with snowplows and sanding cars,

A restored and operational Chicago Surface Line street car at the Illinois Railway Museum. The car, built in 1923, was used mainly on the Broadway-State Street line and was retired from service in 1951. (Courtesy of Frank Hicks.)

though each regular car carried sand distributors as well. For accident or break-downs, derrick and service cars were ready. There were even fancy party cars for charter.

Soon the rapid, if not smooth and quiet, ride of the street cars caused them to soar in preference by the public. They began to spread out in a web that covered the city. At one time Chicago accurately claimed to have the most street railways in the world with over 1,000 miles of track, 700,000,000 paid annual fares (over a billion if transfers are factored in), the most rolling stock and employees, and the longest rides.

To help visualize the street car system think of it as analogous to the human circulatory system. The main lines were laid on the most important streets. They could be considered the arteries. In fact, that was what they were called. The smaller lines branching off would be comparable to the smaller veins and capillaries. Eventually so many street cars were operating that virtually every resident of the city was within walking distance of a stop. The ride would still cost a nickel and included a free transfer if requested. Within two hours that transfer would allow you to transfer to a different line where you could request one more free transfer. You could and many people did use the privilege to make a "jolly day upon the trolley." The terms trolley and street car are generally used interchangeably but actually the trolley is the device which connects the street car motor to the overhead wires. At the end of the line, the motorman and conductor simply had to switch the trolley 180 degrees to be on their way back. Sometimes there was a turntable to accomplish the same thing. Usually the two crew members were assisted by riders or others nearby.

Street cars made travel easier and faster for many reasons. As they were expanded and ridership increased the lines attracted commerce like a magnet attracts iron filings. Arterial and lesser lines soon bristled with businesses of every type. There were butchers and bakers and greengrocers, five and ten cent stores like Kresge's and Woolworth's, lumber and coal yards, hardware and paint stores, appliance dealers, and repair shops. Funeral parlors and, symbolically, auto dealers, filling stations, and mechanic services came along too. There were the few attorneys needed for mundane things like zoning, permits, and probate. Doctors, dentists, churches, barbers and beauty shops, hospitals, restaurants, taverns, and bars were all there. For local public safety, you would find firehouses and police stations. Wasteland marshes were recontoured to create parks with small lakes for boating and fishing. They could be found anywhere along the route or more likely at the end of the line. When mentioning parks, you could take the street car to Wrigley Field on the North Side or Comiskey Park on the South Side. You wouldn't see very good baseball, but Chicagoans are always quick to say, "Wait 'til next year." Or at least you heard it until 2016. Another favorite destination was the Riverview Amusement Park.

The intersection of lines was the perfect place to build very large stores, the most impressive and useful being multi-storied department stores, clones of the most prestigious of the Loop stores: Sears, Roebuck and Co, Mandel Bros., The Fair, and Montgomery Wards. They could accurately be called vertical indoor shopping malls without the long walks through acres of parking lots and hallways. They were also pleasant because the clerks were invariably well-dressed, smiling, polite, and helpful. Elevators were operated by more polite people who always asked, "Floor please?"

Among other important buildings at intersections you might find government offices, business offices, movie palaces, and a dwindling number of vaudeville houses. This is where you could find a bank or savings and loan. The banks would likely be branches of downtown banks. The mutual savings and loans were frequently smaller and more friendly. Often they were funded by ethnic groups to give their neighbors a better chance of obtaining home loans. These centers of commerce were aptly called "Hubs" for indeed they were at the center of a system of spoke-like streets and trolley routes. Street railroads also connected all of Chicago's heavy rail depots and light rail interurban lines as well.

If most people were asked what the main factor was in the decline and disappearance of the street railroads they might blame the auto and truck. That's a logical guess but only a partially correct one as it turns out. As early as 1926, long before travel by auto became the norm, the CCRY was forced into bankruptcy. The main reason was that cap which kept the maximum fare at five cents. The railroads simply could not keep up with increasing maintenance, wages, and cost of replacement cars when they could not raise fares.

The solution to the bankruptcy of the now named Chicago Surface Lines was, ironically, more legislation. The city was given permission to take over the street railways for a bargain price under the name Chicago Transit Authority. The CTA still exists though the old-fashioned street cars are long gone, their tracks either ripped up for scrap or covered by asphalt. The CTA has tried hard to improve things by investing in larger, more comfortable, and faster rolling stock. Older Chicagoans will fondly or not so much recall riding the Green Hornet. It derived its name from the paint colors and possibly because of a popular radio show of the same name. The Green Hornet cars made a difference, but they still had the limitation of having to stay on the tracks. A new CTA car was purchased which was a hybrid of the street car and a bus. It still used overhead power lines but it could be steered a bit around potholes and needed no tracks. Now there are only buses which have the advantage of needing only a single employee to drive and see that fares are paid or multi-ride tickets punched.

Chicago also has an elevated route and a subway which each carries thousands of passengers every day and by definition do not interfere with street traffic. They were also different because they use a "third rail " for power. As the name implies, this was another rail carrying a lethal charge of electricity along the route. To touch it is to be instantly electrocuted. That chance is almost eliminated by having the tracks away from the streets. Relatively new extensions have brought the El to Midway and O'Hare airports

The CTA is no stranger to the problems that keep public transportation a losing proposition. It can and does seek rate hikes from the state legislature, but every time the rates are raised ridership declines. Fares in 2019 ranged from $2.00 full fare, to $1.10 for senior citizens and students and $.25 for a transfer. Crime has come to the CTA, especially to the El where armed robbery and gang violence is increasing. Still it remains popular with the sophisticated young urban population and sports fans of baseball, football, basketball, and ice hockey. And students can take advantage of its relatively modest fares to attend the many fine universities in and around the city. All can avoid the many expenses of owning a car. Indeed, though public transportation has gone through many phases, it is still well-used by millions for getting around town.

The last street car ran down the Wentworth line just sixty years ago filled with reporters and those who were sorry to see them go. Today there are hundreds of thousands of elderly Chicagoans who remember them well. What they used to take for granted as a necessary mundane round trip they made each workday has become nostalgic. The rocking and swaying of the cars, the rolling and shaking of the trucks, the squeal of metal on metal, the smells, dirt, and straps hanging and the constant clanging of the bell have now become memories of the Good Old Days.

3

THE WINDY CITY

CHICAGO POLITICAL CONVENTIONS

You all know how Chicago got its nickname, don't you? Or do you? It's the harsh wind that will sear the city in the summer and when it comes as "the Hawk" during the harsh winters, it will chill you to the bone no matter how layered-up you are. If that's your answer, it might be based on the fact that the wind can be brutal, especially when it blows in from Lake Michigan. But you'd be wrong. Chicago gets its second moniker from the twenty-seven national political conventions which have been held there, more than any other city. The "Windy" comes from the many speeches and addresses mostly self-serving, long, and boring which are a part of every convention. They were often called real "stem-winders" when delegates were exclusively male and all wore pocket watches.

But, why Chicago? One reason was surely its location at the cross-roads of railroads and later improved highways and airports. Chicago had ample hotel accommodations for thousands of convention delegates. There were restaurants of infinite variety. For the highbrow, there was legitimate theater, a world-class art museum, symphony orchestra, and opera. For all the others, there was vaudeville and movies. For all, there were hundreds of bars and taverns. For more sordid entertainment for the jolly fellows from big cities and small towns, the population of loose women soared during the convention nights.

The city was modern and expanding rapidly with a transportation network of streetcars, taxis, and livery coaches to get everyone around comfortably, quickly, and safely. By the 1890s, the city was running on gas and electric power and telephones were common. There were dozens of newspapers to cover the convention events. Above all, there were convention halls for all the delegates to sit and once in a while break the boredom with a show of adolescent exuberance in a demonstration with buttons, signs, hats, and placards.

Chicago's first convention had the most historical significance. In 1860, the upstart Republican Party met to nominate an anti-slavery candidate who had a chance of defeating his opponents. That person was Illinois' favorite-son, candidate Abraham Lincoln, the backwoods country lawyer. He had risen very quickly to national prominence through a series of debates with Stephen Douglas. The site of the convention was the first of three buildings given the name Wigwam. The first Wigwam was in downtown Chicago at the corner of Lake Street and Wacker Drive. It was built in only two months' time and was considered dilapidated almost as soon as it opened. Made entirely of wood, it was no surprise that according to the Chicago Tribune it burned in a "volume of smoke and ashes." In 1892 the Democrats met in the last of the three Wigwams nominating Grover Cleveland for a non-consecutive second term. The Republicans returned to Chicago in 1868 to meet in the short-lived Crosby's Opera House. Ulysses Grant was the candidate nominated. The convention was notable for another reason. It was the first in which black delegates took part.

Two other convention halls have been used but once. In 1888, the Republican Party convened at the brand-new Auditorium Theater designed by the renowned firm of Dankmar Adler and Louis Sullivan. It nominated Benjamin Harrison and Levi Morton. Over the years the Auditorium has been bankrupt and threatened with razing before being purchased by Roosevelt University. It now considered one of the premier performance halls in the world. Among those who have appeared there, John Phillip Sousa, Sarah Bernhart, Anna Pavlova, Franklin Roosevelt, and Booker T. Washington. FDR's cousin, Teddy, made one of the most famous speeches of his career there when, in his quest for a second term, bragged he "felt fit as a bull moose."

Another single use auditorium is the United Center. It replaced the venerable Chicago Stadium where the Chicago Bulls and Blackhawks once played. The 1996 convention nominated the team of Bill Clinton and Al Gore for a second term. The United Center is the only structure still remaining where a national political convention has been held in Chicago. The United Center is the new home of the Bulls and Blackhawks.

The Chicago Stadium was one of the most popular locations for conventions. Built on Chicago's West Side, it saw some famous moments. The Democratic Party met there in 1896, 1932, 1940, and 1944. The 1932 convention was where FDR made an unprecedented trip by air to accept the nomination in person. As he struggled to the rostrum on his steel-braced legs he was greeted with almost rabid cheering. His speech announced the New Deal for the American People to combat "one-third of the nation" out of work.

There was a much less dignified but nevertheless interesting event at the 1944 convention, "The Voice from the Sewer." FDR had thrown the nominating process open to any candidate. If he were nominated and accepted he would be running for a third term, a move that would break with the tradition set by George Washington, Thomas Jefferson, and others. There was no movement in the unsettled crowd, a stalemate. Then suddenly a booming voice from a hidden loudspeaker began to chant "We want Roosevelt! We want Roosevelt!" over and over. It's exactly what the delegates needed and they were instantly on their feet shouting and marching up and down the aisles. Roosevelt was nominated and "graciously accepted." The voice was that of leather-lunged Thomas Garry, Mayor Ed Kelly's Commissioner of Sanitation hidden in the basement with a microphone. The Republicans also came to the stadium in 1932 and 1944 where they named the FDR clone Wendell Wilkie and the New York racket busting district attorney, Thomas E. Dewey respectively. The stadium building was no marvel of architecture but served its purposes well. In 1994 it was torn down and replaced by parking lots for the United Center.

If the Chicago Stadium could be called a "pile of bricks," then the Coliseum was much the opposite. Like the Wigwam, there were eventually three buildings with the name. The Democrats met at the second Coliseum. It had a troubled beginning when the partially completed structure collapsed and had to be rebuilt. When it was finished it was an impressive 300 by 700-foot floor space, twice that of Madison Square Garden. The 1896 convention provided one of the most memorable moments in convention history. William Jennings Bryan, a thirty-six-year-old little regarded former Congressman, rose to make the final address to a deadlocked convention. The culmination caused one of the best-known moments in American political history when Bryan exclaimed "You shall not press down this crown of thorns upon the brow of labor. You shall not crucify mankind on a cross of gold." The speech electrified the delegates who nominated Bryan on the fourth ballot. He went on to lose that election and again in 1900 and once more in 1908.

The Republicans must have liked the Coliseum a great deal for they held an unmatched five consecutive conventions there from 1904–1920. In 1920 another barrier was crossed when women delegates were seated even before they had achieved suffrage. That 1920 convention also saw the fulfillment of a prophecy. The voting was so hopelessly deadlocked that party bosses retired to a room in the Blackstone Hotel to hammer out a deal. The prophecy was that the nomination would be assured in the ". . . middle of the night in a smoke-filled room." The compromise candidate was the malleable and for all intents and purposes unknown senator from Ohio, Warren Gamaliel Harding. When he was offered the nomination on the telephone, he famously paused a moment and then said "I don't know. Let me ask my wife." The stadium was also the site of one of the more curious splinter parties in history. When the party bosses turned their influence from the unpredictable Teddy Roosevelt to the utterly predictable William Howard Taft., TR and his supporters bolted the party. They also met at the stadium in 1912 and 1916. Their ill-fated campaign split the Republican vote, guaranteeing two terms for the Democrat Woodrow Wilson.

The Chicago Fire of 1871 shocked not only Chicagoans but the nation as well. Business leaders were determined to prove the fire had not diminished its position as the nation's convention center as well as its center of commerce. To do this, a group of influential civic leaders created a vision for the most opulent building possible. Some of their names are still well-known; Potter Palmer, Jacob Rosenberg, and Joseph Medill were the officers and on the board were R.T. Crane, Charles Fargo, and Marshall Field. The International (Interstate) Exhibition Hall was a true palace. Built on the lakefront, it was modeled after London's Crystal Palace and constructed of glass and steel. The interior area was an enormous 200 by 800 feet, over three-and-a-half acres, and contained an art museum at the entrance to dispel the thoughts of Chicago as a second city. It hosted two consecutive Republican conventions in 1880 when James G. Garfield and Chester Alan Arthur got the nod. In 1884 the nominees were the ill-fated James F. Blaine and another favorite son, Gen. John A Logan Civil War hero and former congressman and senator.

The hall had a busy life but a short one as was planned. By the 1890s, the hall was several blocks from the lakefront because landfill had been brought in to expand on Daniel Burnham's Plan for Chicago. The site was scheduled to be part of the World's Columbian Exhibition. The exhibition hall was dismantled and a permanent building constructed on the land. Eventually and fittingly it became the Chicago Art Institute, one of the world's most highly regarded fine arts showcases. The Exhibition Hall holds a record that will almost certainly never be equaled or broken, hosting eight conventions.

The International Amphitheater was another popular convention center hosting five meetings in four years. The Republicans had much better luck there nominating former general Dwight Eisenhower in 1952 and 1956. The Democrats also met at the amphitheater those years but had the hopeless task of defeating the popular "Ike." In both elections, their sacrificial lamb candidate was Adlai Stevenson, an intellectual former governor of Illinois. While he was a fine governor, he was utterly colorless and passive and excited exactly no one in the two campaigns.

At least those Democratic conventions were peaceful which certainly couldn't be said of the convention held there in 1968. The street scenes of violence between rioters picking a fight with Chicago police and National

Guard and regular Army troops are still easily remembered. Arson-caused fires and store looting spread across the city's South and West Sides. Even though the nation was all too familiar with scenes of violence in the tumultuous year of 1968, it was still shocking. In the convention hall, speakers condemned the overreaction of the police. A "police riot" it was called. Though it has never been proven that the violence in the streets was planned to disrupt the convention, it certainly did. Mayor Richard J. Daly was furious and offended that such demonstrations were happening in his city and being broadcast live around the world. His rage caused him to issue an order ". . . to shoot to kill arsonists and anyone with a Molotov cocktail . . . and to shoot to maim or cripple anyone looting any stores in our city." The media turned from the convention proceedings to the bloody fights in the streets and the burning city blocks. The convention was a disastrous way to begin a campaign, dooming the ticket of Hubert H. Humphrey and Edmund Muskie.

The amphitheater was located on Chicago's far West Side very near the stockyards and was designed for livestock exhibitions. It quickly became popular with both parties for conventions because it had two innovations other buildings lacked. It was air-conditioned and it provided space for broadcast media. For years it was also the setting for sports and outdoors, travel and auto shows, professional wrestling, and rodeos.

After the terrible violence of 1968, as if the city were tainted, only a single subsequent convention was held in the City-By-The-Lake. For twenty-eight years, the longest period in its history, no convention was held in Chicago. After the Democratic convention in 1996 neither party has chosen Chicago again, an additional twenty-one years have gone by—a total of almost half a century.

For more than a century, Chicago proved not only a convenient city for political conventions but has always provided ample, dependable and often imposing locations and a labor pool which could handle such large meetings easily. In these places, no matter the party or the events, sometimes routine and mundane and at others unpredictable, exciting, and divisive, decisions were made that determined American history.

4

THE CITY BY THE LAKE

CHICAGO'S FRONT YARD

If you're just lucky enough to approach O'Hare Airport on a clear day and on the lucky side of the plane, you will catch a spellbinding sight. Stretched out below you is the Chicago skyline, the finest in the world, set against the azure blue of Lake Michigan. Look carefully: you will see a necklace of green set with small white gems. Even frequent fliers take the time for a glimpse. What you're seeing is Chicago's Front Yard, its incomparable lakefront. You'll only be able to see the sight for a few moments but the image will remain—guaranteed!

From Evanston on the north to Jackson Park on the south it stretches twenty-six miles with fifteen miles of swimming beaches set aside for the people of the city and visitors from all around the world. Those tiny "gems" you saw are the crown jewels of the lakefront and some of the most brilliant, delightful, and popular places anywhere. From world-famous museums and a fine arts gallery to athletic fields and restful fishing spots, it provides something for everyone, judging by the tens of millions of annual visitors who share the parks.

If it strikes your thoughts just right, it wouldn't be wrong to also dub the lakefront "Chicago's Theme Park." Nor would you be the first to think it. The best theme parks operate on the principles of taking people away from their everyday routines, to relax, laugh, and have fun. If they're really well-planned they can help you learn. Theme parks should be clean and safe and offer pleasure for all. It's not a perfect analogy, but it's close. Perhaps the greatest difference is that the lakefront's open space is there for you to enjoy for free. There is no eighty-dollar daily admission and no overpriced meals. It will be crowded at times but the crowds have square miles in which to spread out. You'll find no costly parking fees, no crowded trams to help you cross hundred-acre parking lots, no passes that need to be presented, no security checks except at buildings. Believe it or not, you just walk in where you want to be. You might have to pay for parking but the area is well-served by inexpensive public transportation.

Theme parks "price-out" many a family who can't afford the expensive transportation, lodging, meals, and admission costs, no matter how badly they want to go. Here you can bring a picnic lunch and enjoy a leisurely day in a park or at one of the many beaches and then return to your own home the same day. The only costs will be those of getting there and those of building admissions and rides you might want to add to your day.

Let's take the analogy one step further though it's an unexpected one. Every theme park by its nature, or lack of it, drastically changes the landscape on which it's built. As natural as it looks from the air and close up on the ground every acre of Chicago's lakefront is artificial, land created by the hand of man. In 1871, today's lakefront was part of Lake Michigan's deep waters. After the Great Fire of that year, Chicago was faced with the task of disposing of millions of cubic yards of rubble. Transportation was primitive and would have taken years to remove if the lake were not so close. The lakefront was nearly all vacant land, just sand dunes, and grasses. Developers also quickly saw the advantage of expanding Chicago's downtown acreage for commercial purposes. Over the years more and more landfill was disposed of. In order to get rid of it effectively, barges took most of it out to deep water to dump. There was no EPA to seek a court order to halt the work. Eventually, the original shoreline became as much as a half-mile west of its present location.

To dump debris in the close-by lake took absolutely no vision at all. It was unquestioned by almost everyone. If there were a vision, it was to decide what types of industrial and commercial businesses would be built there. The first was the Illinois Central Railroad which built a large train yard to transfer cargoes and service equipment.

Strictly a business vision perfect for a city on the make. That is until the real dreamers came along to begin a long legal fight between the visionaries and those who valued the real estate for profit. Our nation is rife with examples in which greed and profit won their way. This time the goal of preservation had powerful supporters with great wealth and political clout.

A. Montgomery Ward began the store and mail-order business of his own name which grew in size until it was surpassed only by another Chicago retail giant, Sears and Roebuck. Ward gathered many like himself who opposed a lakefront swallowed by commerce and they campaigned against industrialization. City politicians and business leaders surrendered and built their factories and stores elsewhere.

In 1909, Chicago landscape architect Daniel Burnham issued his Plan for Chicago. It was exactly what was needed to give hazy idealism a practical design. The Burnham Plan stretched twenty-six miles along Lake Michigan, an unique acreage when you compare it with a connected municipal parkland system anywhere else.

There are four major parks, Lincoln Park, Grant Park, Burnham Park, and Jackson Park from north to south. Of the four, Lincoln Park is the largest and considered by many the most beautiful. It runs seven amazing miles and contains more than 12,000 acres. It is Chicago's oldest park partly because it began as open space containing the city cemetery. Fear of contamination from frequent plagues of dysentery, typhoid, and cholera caused all but one of the burials to be exhumed and moved to other cemeteries well outside the city limits at the time, including Rosehill and Graceland. Inside the park's boundaries are the Chicago Historical Museum, Peggy Notebaert Nature Museum, Lincoln Park Zoo, the Lincoln Park Conservatory, and the Caldwell Lilly Pool. Add the commemorative sculptures and you have many chances to learn. Those are important cultural opportunities, but it's far from all Lincoln Park has for you to enjoy. The friendly confines of Lincoln Park have a golf course, an archery range, indoor and outdoor sports facilities, fishing spots, and even a special park for man's best friend.

Grant Park has become second in popularity despite being one-fourth the area. Its location at the edge of the city's most exclusive shops, stores, restaurants, and offices between Michigan Ave. and Lake Shore Drive ensures that. After years of protest and political in-fighting, several acres of the park were excavated and two immense subterranean parking garages were built which together have room for over three thousand cars. When the garages were completed, they were recovered and restored to green space. Near the park is another surprising engineering achievement— a commuter railroad. It's the Chicago, South Shore, and South Bend. The station is recessed below grade-level and largely invisible unless you know where to look because it runs through the lakefront area fully below ground level. It's all-electric so it is virtually silent and pollution free.

Speaking of controversial uses of the park, the second Mayor Daley of Chicago, Richard M., had an idea he liked. At the turn of the twenty-first century, he was able to build Millennium Park. Maligned by many at first partly because of an immense walk-in chrome sculpture satirically nicknamed "The Bean," its surface gives endless fun-house distortions and is particularly popular with honeymooners from the world over. It's become a favorite of the people and proves politicians sometimes have a vision, too. There's also an outdoor concert theater and wading pool especially popular with children of all ages. Grant Park is where you will find most of the lakefront's most iconic landmarks including Navy Pier

The sculpture from Millennium Park nicknamed "The Bean."

and Kate Buckingham's stunning and colorful fountain, a tribute to her husband Clarence. The band shell has summer Pops' symphony concerts, not to mention less high-brow fare such as The Chicago Blues Festival and Lollapalooza.

It's gone through boom and abandonment more than once so it's encouraging to find Navy Pier at its peak once again. It's been a military training center and the first site of The University of Illinois' Chicago campus. When the Big U moved to another location, the Pier was abandoned and quickly became a near ruin. Now its central location makes it immensely popular. You can walk or bike around it for exercise, go on a tall-ship, dinner cruise, or fast jet boat. You can eat at fancy places or at Billy Goat's, the descendant of Billy Goat's Tavern downtown most associated with the now useless "curse" on the Cubs. There's a giant Ferris wheel for a commanding view of the city and lake. (The first such device was built for the Columbian Exhibition in Chicago by George Ferris). For drama and comedy, the pier offers the appropriately named "Chicago Shakes" Shakespearean theater and an improv comedy troop. Navy Pier is host to Chicago's two most popular events. The Independence Day pyrotechnics and the August Air and Water show typically draw orderly crowds estimated at 1,000,000 each.

If you walk, jog, ride, or Rollerblade, you'll next come to the appropriately named Burnham Park which has one of several high-rent yacht basins along the lakefront. Between Grant Park and Burnham Park is Chicago's famed museum campus and the home of a world class art school. In reality, two of the buildings are not museums but all are filled with knowledge and opportunities to learn. The three main structures are the John Shedd Aquarium, The Adler Planetarium, and the Field Museum. Both the Shedd and the Field were established through the philanthropy of Marshall Field and his protege. Max Adler, another successful businessman funded the nation's first planetarium in 1930. On Michigan Avenue is the Chicago Art Institute, one of the world's finest art museums and home of a world class art school.

Not all ideas are good, as some of Mayor Richard M.'s haven't been. The most glaring example is along Lake Shore Drive and all the more visible to hundreds of thousands, especially on game days. In order to keep the Chicago Bears from following up on a threat to bolt to the suburbs for a better facility, Daley agreed to the cheapest and most ugly adaptation possible. The most common reaction is that it resembles a flying saucer which has come to rest on the Neo-Classic columns of Soldier Field. This one almost certainly will never be loved like The Bean. Much to his outrage, Daley's change caused the city's Landmark Commission to revoke the site's landmark status.

There's one more striking structure to pass before you leave Burnham Park. Few will call it beautiful or striking. The word you might hear most often is practical. McCormick Place is by far Chicago's largest assembly hall. It's the site of a great variety of trade shows, auto shows, sports and outdoor shows, and representative assemblies. Following the Lake Shore Path farther south you come upon less spectacular but still beautiful park land for sports and group gatherings. There are beaches at 57th and 63rd Streets. Nearby is Promontory Point, a stone covered landfill built specifically for Big Band performances during the Century of Progress Fair. Now it is a popular place to view the incomparable Chicago skyline and have a conversation amongst sculpted fire pits.

Jackson Park contains the remnants of one of the earliest and easily most spectacular and successful world's fairs. It was literally brilliant as well because hundreds of its whitewashed buildings were all brightly lit by millions of electric lights giving the World's Columbian Exhibition of 1893 its second name "The White City." In the early part of the twentieth century, the site was a popular amusement park also named White City.

Jackson Park has recently become the center of a difficult struggle over a proposal to locate the three-billion-dollar Obama Presidential Center there. This is an unusual battle in that all groups agree on the belief that the Obama legacy belongs in the city. The location at Jackson Park is the problem. Lakefront protectionists see it as a degradation of the century and a quarter dedication to the concept of an open lakefront created by Daniel Burnham. Also alarmed at the location are Jackson Park community agencies which fear the inevitable impact the gentrification brought by the project will have on neighborhood residents. Allied against them are developers who see limitless opportunities and City Hall which wants it as a complement to the nearby Museum of Science and Industry to create a campus to rival that at Grant Park. It also desires the prestige and income the center will generate. City Hall clout was also behind the location because it was favored by former Mayor Rahm Emanuel. The fight is now in the federal courts and there is a new mayor, so time will tell the outcome.

Nearly all venues at the Columbian Exhibition were lightly built to save time and money and minimize problems with restoration of the lakefront. The Beaux Arts exhibition hall that was The Palace of Fine Arts was not one of them. It was built to last with a masonry core. The building was restored once, only to fall into ruin again. For years it deteriorated from lack of purpose and maintenance until it was indeed torn down. In another example of Chicago's commitment to learning, it was replaced by today's identical and permanent hall thanks to the leadership and philanthropy of one of the city's wealthiest business executives, Julius Rosenwald, president of Sears, Roebuck & Co., who donated the astonishing sum of $5,000,000 for the project. The Museum of Science and Industry is now the largest science museum in the world. There you'll find the legendary captured German Submarine U-505, one of the largest model railroads in the world, a replica coal mine, and days' worth of other visiting.

Stay on the Trail and you'll find two more harbors, a nine-hole golf course, and at the south end of the bicycle trail, the former South Shore Country Club, now a cultural center and culinary school. Just inside the old gates of the center is the stable for Chicago's Mounted Police Patrol. Not too far away is the exquisite Osaka Japanese Garden originally found in Japan's depiction of its culture in 1893. The Frederick Law Olmstead landscape plan for the fair included the grand Midway Plaisance and it still runs through the campus of The University of Chicago, one of the world's great seats of learning.

Two other important and successful fairs can be found in the lake front's past. The earlier was the 1933–34 Century of Progress World's

Fair celebrating Chicago's first century of, well, progress. Held mostly in Burnham Park, this one was so marvelous it was held over for a second year. Its executive manager was Major Lenox Lohr, who guided the fair to financial success for its backers and a much-needed boost to Chicago's confidence. The city invested nothing in the fair for it had nothing in those early years of the Great Depression. It provided so great a boost to Chicago's morale that it was given recognition by one of the four stars on Chicago's flag. (The others are for Ft. Dearborn, The Great Fire, and The World's Columbian Exhibition. The two wavy blue lines represent the Chicago River and Lake Michigan.)

In 1948, the same Major Lohr oversaw the preparation and presentation of the Railroad Fair. Largely an exhibition in which the railroads gave themselves a pat on the back it was nevertheless fascinating and educational. It featured a musical pageant created just for the fair titled "Wheels a-Rollin," which used a cast of hundreds to entertain millions with the depiction of the history of transportation in America often using original rolling stock. Like the Century of Progress, the Railroad Fair proved so popular that it was held a year longer than planned.

A series of artificial islands (more landfill) was planned for the 1933 fair but only Northerly Island was actually built due to lack of funding and time. In 1948, it opened as Chicago's beloved lakefront airport, the small but busy airport named Meigs Field. The field was a thorn in the side of Mayor Daley II as he saw it as competition for Midway and O'Hare. Frustrated by rules that required the city to petition for permission to close the airfield, in 2003 he decided to defy the Friends of Meigs and the FAA by ordering a middle of the night raid by city bulldozers which ripped great X's across the runway making it unusable and stranding seventeen small aircraft. Now the island is what the mayor envisioned, an open space restored with grasses and other plant life to give the city a glimpse of how the Illinois prairie looked before there was a Chicago. You can walk the path and find a peaceful, if windy, park of a different kind.

Lake Michigan has its moods. It can be inspiring on a sunny day with puffy cumulus clouds to give definition to the tall sky. Other times clouds and fog will confound your mind. It has a measurable tide. With enough wind from the right direction it will build an enjoyable surf you can hear or swim in. That the big lake has moods assumes that it is capricious, changing almost instantly without warning. Due to its long and narrow geological shape, it can produce fearsome and deadly storms called gales by meteorologists but "White Hurricanes or "November Witches" by sailors. Great storms are unusual but not rare. More uncommon is another deadly lake phenomenon—a "seiche" in which a squall can produce a significant freshwater tidal wave. As with a tsunami, it can travel hundreds of invisible, unfelt miles until it piles up against a shore. One of the largest recorded did just that along the beaches and shoreline from the Chicago River to Wilmette in June of 1954. One of the favorite fishing spots for anglers is the long breakwater into the lake at Lincoln Park. Fishermen can easily walk out hundreds of feet to deep water on it. This sunny day the seiche came in ten feet high without warning. Today a cable runs the length of the breakwater but there was nothing in 1954 to be grabbed. All of the fishermen were swept into the water and eight of them drowned. Besides the reason for the beauty of the lakefront there is another popular but unproven benefit it gives the city. In its long history Chicago has only had one tornado and an F-0 at that. The theory is that the cool waters of the lake disrupt the warm/cool confluences that cause the violent, deadly storms elsewhere. The same lake water makes the lakefront cooler in torrid summers and warmer in Arctic-like winters.

People come to the lakefront specifically to be in the parks and houses of knowledge it contains, to enjoy its natural beauty, entertain themselves in recreation, or to just relax in Chicago's Front Yard. It's a vital gift to all the world that this land has come to be preserved and maintained.

5

A CHICAGO LAKEFRONT GEM

THE MUSEUM OF SCIENCE AND INDUSTRY

The Chicago lakefront has three of the world's very best museums. Two of them, the Field Museum of Natural History and the Chicago Art Institute, are on the museum campus near the Shedd Aquarium and the Adler Planetarium in Grant Park. That location makes them more available and therefore more popular.

To the author, there is a discernible difference between being popular and being interesting. The third of the great museums is the Museum of Science and Industry (MS&I) which just happens to be the world's largest science museum containing an awesome 300,000 square feet of exhibit halls, offices, labs, maintenance facilities, and storage space. Even popular, interesting, and huge don't account for the author's fascination with the big building. Please indulge him for a time as he tries to explain. When his family made its trips to the MS&I, they would have to take their time because there were no expressways. The first thing the author noticed was the wide and steep stairs to the main hall. Even as young boys, he and his cousins would have to climb it in impatient stages to let parents catch up. Inside the rotunda, eyes couldn't avoid being drawn upward by the four full-scale aircraft. He marveled at how thin the cables were that held them fast and felt a little unsure about walking under them.

In the earliest visits, he tagged along with his parents. When he was seven or so, he had been given a brand-new Westclox wristwatch when

The U-505 German submarine inside the Museum of Science and Industry. (Courtesy of the Museum of Science and Industry.)

he learned to tell time. Parents had a different mindset then so he was allowed to wander on his own after they had paid the extra fee for the coal mine and later the U-505. Strict orders were given as to where and when to meet to get their picnic lunch from a rental locker so the family could eat in one of the dining halls.

Is it possible that a boy can be born with a nostalgia gene? One hasn't been charted so far, but even at the tender age of seven or eight, the author found himself always returning to walk "The Streets of Yesterday" and the nearby hall filled with old vehicles. He walked through the human heart with its loud heartbeat. You get the idea and this chapter is about the MS&I, not about the author's memories so we'll get on with things.

The MS&I structure derives from the oldest of the three great museum structures. It dates from what some consider the most spectacular world's fair of them all, The World's Columbian Exhibition of 1893. Then the building was The Palace of Fine Arts. All the other exhibit locations were built fast, cheap, and expendable. A year after the fair they were all gone except the Palace. It had a brick core below the canvas and Plaster of Paris

The University of Chicago. (Courtesy of the Wikimedia Commons public domain.)

on the facade. The plan was that after the fair it would be made into a permanent museum honoring the great exhibition as the fair landscape architect Frederic Law Olmstead had intended. It never realized that use, but it did become the first home of the Field Museum. When the Field moved to its new home downtown, the former palace languished and deteriorated with no plans for use. Had it been farther from the lakefront it may well have been torn down as an eyesore at this stage. The city was so embarrassed by its dilapidated appearance that the South Parks Commission secured a five-million-dollar bond issued to refurbish the old place for a trade school and sculpture hall/studios for Lorado Taft, a professor of sculpture at the nearby University of Chicago and one of America's premier sculptors. That plan too lagged and the building lost focus for a third time.

Located in Jackson Park near some of Chicago's most prestigious neighborhoods at the time and meant to complement the Oxford and Cambridge architectural style of the next-door University of Chicago campus the old place looked like what it was, a vacant pile with no purpose. It certainly had a charmed life, because it had its best years still to come. One of its Hyde Park neighbors was almost certainly the wealthiest man in Chicago at the time. Julius Rosenberg was part-owner and president of the city's biggest retail engine, Sears, Roebuck & Co., which was in its best earning years. Rosenberg had traveled to Europe many times and had become very interested in the concept of a science-only museum he found at the Deutsches Museum in Munich, Germany. His admiration for it caused him to make up his mind to establish just such a museum in America. After all, his reasoning went, there was no country among the world's nations which had prospered more from science than the United States. His mind may have even been made up more certainly by his familiarity with the enormous exhibit space available in his own neighborhood.

All the project needed was money and lots of it. If there was anything Julius Rosenberg had a lot of, it was money. Some people would call this a serendipitous junction of supply and demand. Whatever you call it Rosenberg began to fund it. He initially pledged an enormous sum— three million dollars to rebuild the old structure from the ground up so it would not rot away again. He also instructed his architects not to use any contemporary style for the exterior, but to restore the wonderful Beaux Arts facade of the original palace.

Rosenberg was a prominent member of the exclusive Chicago Commercial Club which was made up of other members of Chicago's wealthy elite. He prevailed on three of them for funds to finance a museum staff and begin its collections. Among his angels were Avery Sewell, the president of Montgomery Ward; Henry Crown, the founder of Material Services Corporation and board member of General Dynamics; and Joseph Regenstein, president and owner of Velsical Chemicals, producer of copious amounts of DDT, and the future subject of Rachel Carson's *Silent Spring.*

The board of directors of the new museum hired its first managing director, Waldemar Kaempffert, the science editor of *The New York Times.* Kaempffert immediately began to hire staff and make acquisitions to help the MS&I rival its counterpart in Germany. The museum opened in three stages, the first in 1933 and the final in 1940 as collections were acquired and prepared for exhibition. Most Chicagoans know the year of 1933 as a pivotal one in the history of the city for it was when the marvelous Century of Progress World's Fair opened. This time the old Palace of Fine Arts was not the center of the fair but was, in fact, several miles south in Jackson Park. Still, millions who come to the fair made their way to the new museum they had heard about.

The Museum of Science and Industry isn't a museum like the Field with exhibits displaying extinct animals and human history so ancient that the visitors with a common level of education have little chance of relating to it. Similarly, many who come to the Art Institute for the first time see only paintings, not levels of meaning and the techniques of geniuses. The planetarium shows them a cosmos so vast they have trouble understanding what that means for their everyday lives. Even the Shedd Aquarium with its incredible displays of exotic sea creatures is overwhelming and soon one fish starts to look like another. Call it fish fatigue.

But the Museum of Science and Industry is filled with familiar machinery, tools, vehicles, and scientific discoveries that allow them to interact and understand. There's a coal mine for them to learn from. There is Coleen Moore's fabulous Fairy Palace which they can spiral around to see the working fountains and miniature electric lights. The aircraft, agricultural implements, tools and machines, and a chick hatchery, are all things visitors may be able to personally relate to or have a living memory of. Manufacturing, electronics, communications, transportation, medical, chemical, anatomical, and astronomical, there seems to be no end.

Several of the MS&I oldest exhibits came from the Century of Progress. To mention only one, let's use the coal mine. It is not a model or a replica. It is the real deal, the former Old Ben #10, a southern Illinois bituminous deep shaft mine. Imported to the MS&I were its winding gears and elevator, its original mine train, and replica subterranean tunnels and shafts. There's a cramped room where you learn about mining techniques and the dangers of collapsing tunnels, floods, and

A pre-WWII racing plane from the Musuem of Science and Industry entrance hall. (Courtesy of the Wikimedia Commons public domain.)

deadly methane gas. They used to get the young version of the author every time when they exploded a container of methane.

Over its eighty-five years, the MS&I has become world renowned for some of its "newer" exhibits which are now classics. The constantly growing and updated 3500 s.f. model railroad can be best taken in from the mezzanine by visitors. The Foucault Pendulum hangs from the four-story ceiling and still sways slowly to prove the Earth rotates. The somewhat hidden and surely creepy "body slices," another acquisition from the '33 Fair, still take up room in one of the staircases

Two of the most massive exhibits deserve special mention. The first is the entire three-unit articulated Burlington R.R.'s showpiece Pioneer

Zephyr which set a speed record by averaging 77 mph between Denver and Chicago and reaching a maximum speed of 112 mph, spelling the effective end of steam power in the railroad industry.

The other must be the largest single exhibit acquired by any museum anywhere and moved to its exhibit space in one piece. This is the fabled German submarine U-505 captured on the high seas during WWII. It was towed through the Great Lakes to the lakeshore across Lake Shore Drive from the museum in 1955. Crossing the Drive was one of the most delicate and difficult moving projects in history until that time. Many years later when inspections showed serious environmental damage to both the U-boat and the Zephyr, the museum launched a massive fund raising effort which allowed both exhibits to be brought within the walls of the museum for permanent protection.

Director Kaempffert resigned over management issues with the president of the board. If a museum such as the MS&I's can ever say to be complete it reached the end of its three-stage development plan in 1940. After that, it entered a sort of Limbo with no executive willing or capable enough to steer it with confidence and vision. This indecision ended in 1948 when the museum board hired Major Lenox Lohr to be its new president. Lohr came with an impressive resume and a proven record of success in running complicated enterprises. He had been the executive director of the Century of Progress Exhibition, bringing order out of chaos. He accomplished the seemingly impossible by staging one of the great fairs and bringing it in under budget with a modest profit for its investors. When that feat was complete, Lohr was hired by NBC Radio to be its President. Again he excelled, resigning only after a dispute with NBC over its lack of news broadcasting and blind spot when it came to adopting the new medium of television.

He seemed to be the perfect fit for the MS&I position and so it turned out. Lohr immediately saw that the museum languished for lack of forward motion and depleted funding. His vision was to forge partnerships with local manufacturing companies. The museum would consult them in planning a new exhibit related to their field and they would get brand recognition for their financial support. This new path may have been expedient but it did not sit well with more than a few museum staff and some directors who felt the new partnerships threatened the integrity of the museum.

Nevertheless, the concept proved effective and large amounts of cash began to flow from retail, manufacturing, pharmaceutical, transportation, and scientific sources among others. Not only did the influx of money help defray the enormous costs of administration, research, maintenance and exhibit preparation, planning, and installation, it also allowed the MS&I to acquire expensive new exhibits such as the U-505 and the Pioneer Zephyr and to refurbish others such as the multi-year updating and expansion of the Great American Train Story.

Any museum which has been around as long as the MS&I must make decisions about its exhibits that creates a delicate balance. If you keep too many of the "Old Favorites," your museum becomes stale. Such a reputation will cause new visitors to go elsewhere and give old visitors less reason to come back to see what's different. Change too many of the favorites and while you will add new visitors, you may well lose your dependable repeat visitors who resent their absence. A museum dedicated to the past has it easier. If it doesn't change much it has a better chance of remaining relevant. A museum like the MS&I had no such luxury. If it doesn't change with the times it will become irrelevant quickly. Lohr set the museum on a course of continual review and updated the exhibits to reflect changes in scientific thought and achievement.

If you returned to the MS&I after many years you would find a myriad of changes, most of them welcome, all of them necessary. Admission to the museum had been free for its first fifty-five years, but gradually an admission fee increased to its present $18.00. Parking is an additional $22.00 for a full day. To avoid the parking fee there are three CTA bus routes which reach the museum from Downtown. The traditional entrance from the massive stairway into the rotunda has had to change as well. Now there is a glass-topped atrium similar to that at the Louvre which accommodates ticket sales, museum orientation, and a fine gift shop and book store.

On your return, you would notice the updating of many exhibits. The familiar walk-through heart is now three-dimensional and interactive. The

MS&I was always popular for its preponderance of hands-on exhibits. That trend has only been increased. A visitor will find the Crown Space Center has the actual Apollo Mercury 7 space capsule which orbited the moon, Scott Carpenter's Mercury-Atlas 7 spacecraft, and an interactive Mars Rover. There's also a lunar module trainer and a life-size mock-up of Space Shuttle *Atlantis*. A major addition is the new OminiMax theater with an aluminum dome creating true surround-sound.

Regenstein Hall of Science has been modernized with demonstrations such as "Fast Forward" which shares how technology can change the world. "Reusable City" lets all interact in learning about how to combat pollution and climate change. "Future Energy Chicago" is a new exhibit to boost creative, alternative thinking on resources, housing, and the future of Chicago. Commercial sponsorship has created Allstate Court in which a visitor can find a study of tornado formation through means of a forty-foot-tall waterspout, a tsunami tank and traditional exhibits, a Tesla coil, a Wimshurst machine, and a replica of "Newton's Cradle."

The youngest visitors haven't been ignored. For their learning there is the "Idea Factory," a water table play area, and the "Circus," featuring the fascinating old dioramas of a three-ring circus with animated figures. Just the thing to draw the interest of toddlers. Kids also find captivating the new "Swiss Jolly Ball," the world's largest pinball machine made entirely of salvaged materials.

One fine tradition has been continued in the Christmas Around the World pageant. It started back in 1942 to boost WWII Allied nations' ties. Today it has more than fifty trees decorated as they would be in different nations with costumed actors to increase the realism.

In its ninth decade of combining teaching and entertainment, the place of the Chicago Museum of Science and Industry is secure as the southernmost piece of the extended lakefront museum campus along Lake Shore Drive. It may take a little longer to get there but that doesn't prevent millions of first-time visitors and old-time regulars from making the trip. The term "unique" is regrettably misunderstood and misused in America in the twenty-first century, but it is perfectly applied to describe this great "Gem of the Lake Front."

THE LAKEFRONT LEGACY
OF LENOX LOHR

Any knowledgeable Chicagoan can roll off the names of lakefront legends such as Montgomery Ward, Marshall Field, John G. Shedd, Dankmar Adler, Kate Buckingham, Daniel Burnham, and Lenox Lohr. And whom? Lohr? What's named after him along arguably the most magnificent city lakefront anywhere? The regrettable answer—nothing is. The others made big splashes with big money, big buildings, big, incomparable visions of landscapes and, appropriately in the case of Mrs. Buckingham, a big fountain.

Chicago's lakefront owes at least as much to Lenox Lohr as it does to any of these bigwigs, but the temporal and lasting structures he guided and inspired bear others' names. He'd certainly not be so neglected if there were a Lohr Museum of Science and Industry or a Lohr Convention and Exhibition Hall to name-drop two. And the author could do some further name-dropping by mentioning the Century of Progress and Railroad Fairs. So, what happened to the name of Lenox Lohr? Let's find out.

Lenox Riley Lohr was born in Washington, D.C. in 1891. He graduated with a mechanical engineering degree from Cornell University in 1916 and entered the US Army Corps of Engineers. He had a distinguished military career in WWI including earning a Silver Star for gallantry in the Meuse-Argonne Offensive and rising from the rank of second lieutenant to that of major. In the peacetime army, he displayed his organizational skills by serving as the executive secretary of the Society of Military Engineers and editing its journal.

Major Lohr resigned from the military in 1929 when he was hired to head the new Chicago World's Fair which came to be much better known as the Century of Progress Fair. Lohr was hired by Rufus Dawes, the head of the Fair's investors and brother of Vice-president Charles Dawes. It is likely that Dawes knew of Lohr's talents since they both served in the relatively small Corps of Engineers during The Great War. Major Lohr's job was to be the exhibition's general manager, what we might today call a CEO. The Century of Progress is, of course, legendary not only because of its phenomenal popularity and notoriety, think scandalous fan-dancing Sally Rand, but also because it ran two seasons and, almost without precedent, re-paid all its private investors (No public money was available during those worst years of the Great Depression), even closing with a small surplus. It is even recognized by one of the stars on the Chicago flag. Count this as exhibit number one in the case for the Lohr Legacy.

Even before the great fair ended, Major Lohr had entered negotiations with David Sarnoff and was subsequently hired as president of NBC Radio in 1935. He helped guide the network toward some of its most influential and dominant years. He also oversaw NBC's earliest

Flag of Chicago. (Courtesy of the Wikimedia Commons public domain.)

experiment with television. In an April 1939 article, he was quoted in the Cornell *Daily Sun*, "The greatest future of television lies in the almost unlimited potentialities of television . . . It is believed that it will prove a strong social and educational force in the country." It's an interesting quote because the major doesn't mention the medium's powerful role in entertainment. During his tenure, he recognized the challenges of competition from CBS by championing an end to NBC's ban on transcribed programming and urging his network to acknowledge and emulate the popular success of CBS' news programming.

The year 1940 saw NBC, Sarnoff, and Major Lohr well involved in anti-trust litigation with the FCC over the network's domination of the airwaves by controlling both the NBC Red and Blue Networks. Eventually this led to the agreement to sell off the Red Network—the future ABC. Approaching the age of fifty, and perhaps understandably weary of network broadcasting tensions, Major Lohr returned to Chicago, again at the behest of his mentor Rufus Dawes. This time Lohr would create a more lasting contribution to the lakefront than the Century of Progress, by now just a memory, if a recent one. In 1940 he was hired to replace Dawes as the president of the Museum of Science and Industry.

His appointment was a rescue mission, really. In 1940 the museum was housed in the 1892 relic of the Columbian Exhibition, that Chicago fair before the Century of Progress. It was struggling for inspiration even though, thanks to the 1920's influence of Julius Rosenwald, it had adopted a new name and identity inspired by museums in Europe. His hiring to head the museum was a perfect match for his gifted engineering, business, and management talents. Major Lohr, knowing the lakefront so well, recognized its inherent strengths, located on Lake Shore Drive in the heart of the vibrant Hyde Park and University of Chicago cultures, set in one of Daniel Burnham's gems, Jackson Park, and housed in the massive, unmistakable, Beaux Arts edifice which had been upgraded all around by grants from Rosenwald.

It is important to understand at this juncture that Major Lohr had just ended a five-year career at NBC, the major radio network where he constantly dealt with the antithesis of the past. If he was anything other than a masterful executive at NBC or the Century of Progress, he was a supremely successful promoter. His vision for the Museum of Science and Industry was as clear as it was adroit—a museum devoted to the contemporary and the future, not lashed to the past. Major Lohr quickly implemented his goal by establishing novel partnerships with commercial interests. In exchange for generous funding, the museum created exhibits which instructed in both science and industry.

During his twenty-eight years as president, the Museum of Science and Industry became one of the most popular, highly regarded, and imitated in the world. Certainly, nearly everyone who has lived near or in Chicago has been to the museum at least once. Among those exhibits that Lohr brought are several of its best-known, best-loved, and longest-lived. The mine exhibit was there before Major Lohr's time. However, it bears his imprint for it was transferred directly from the Century of Progress. The Christmas Around the World pageant and display began in 1942 as a way to emphasize the unity of the Allies in WWII. The colossal Santa Fe model railroad layout came in 1943. In 1949, Major Lohr had occasion to visit with silent movie legend, Colleen Moore. According to Moore, Lohr so charmed her she agreed to allow her fabulous Fairy Castle to become one of the most beloved of exhibits. In 1952 the Walk-through Human Heart was added. In 1954 the supreme promoter engineered the passage of the famous "captured on the high-seas by daring rescue" German submarine U-505 from Lake Michigan across Lake Shore Drive into prominent dry-dock display outside the museum. The spectacle was featured in *Life* magazine and elsewhere throughout the nation's media. So, let Major Lohr's re-creation of the Museum of Science and Industry serves as exhibit two in the case for his Lakefront Legacy.

What was next for the organizer extraordinaire? That's an interesting question with a memorable answer. At the request of no less than thirty-nine major rail lines to stage a testament to the role a century of railroads played in America, in just five months, Major Lohr directed the creation of a show, to quote its publicity, "Unlike Any Other." He artfully derailed his employer's wishes to make the fair a tribute to railroads exclusively to the history of all transportation in America from ox-drawn wagon to the most up-to-date, diesel-powered streamliners.

While the show did showcase American railroads, it was also a great spectacle highlighted by the memorable "Wheels-A-Rolling" pageant complete with an original musical score, over a hundred participants and a collection of over a hundred pieces of operating historical vehicles which will never be duplicated. Despite and perhaps partly because of the fair's well-publicized frantic creative pace and risk of attempting to have so many attractions, it was a huge success, drawing 2.5 million visitors the first year. Echoing the Century of Progress, the Chicago Railroad Fair was held for a second year, surpassing the first year in attendance. And true to Lohr's reputation, it repaid its loans. Mark this as exhibit three for Major Lohr. There's more, though.

For obvious reasons, Major Lohr had been a member of the Chicago Fair and Exhibition Corporation for several years. In July of 1955, he was unanimously elected chairman of its successor, the Metropolitan Fair and Exposition Authority. Other members of the board read like a Who's Who of Chicago movers and shakers: Col. Henry Crown, George Halas, James McCahey, Patrick Sullivan, and Arthur Wirtz. Ex-officio members were Gov. William Stratton and the first Mayor Daley. The causes for the consensus choice was obvious. Not only did Major Lohr have a proven record of bringing complicated projects to realization and under budget, he had a vision the others didn't and acknowledged by their choice. Certainly having observed for twenty years Chicago's major role in exhibitions from auto shows to political conventions, he recognized the limitations of the existing venues, the Chicago Stadium, and the International Amphitheater. He saw the developing Chicago expressway system with major junctions so near the former wonderlands he had directed. What better way, he must have thought, to bring to Chicago's incomparably glorious lakefront which he loved so much, not just a transitory exhibition, but a unique, new showplace where millions would be drawn for generations to come?

Major Lohr had already been active in Springfield securing legislation to enable and fund an exhibition hall capable of housing the largest conventions, trade shows, and entertainments. Success for the hall's approval and construction were greatly aided by it being dedicated to

Col. Robert McCormick, publisher of *The Chicago Tribune*, a canny bit of marketing. Once again, it would belie Major Lohr's influence, but surely that inspiration brought a great deal of recognition and support from the self-proclaimed "World's Greatest Newspaper." And so the original McCormick Place came to be known as exhibit number four for the Lakefront Legacy of Lenox Lohr.

There were still other instances of Major Lohr's contributions to Chicago's prosperity. While there is no direct evidence that he was involved, Major Lohr was chair of the Illinois Higher Education Commission from 1954-1959 during the period when the University of Illinois changed its location from restrictive Navy Pier to its present campus. He was also responsible for the fund-raising which saved and restored Jane Addam's Hull House.

During all these activities Major Lohr continued as president of the Museum of Science and Industry until his sudden death from a heart attack on May 30, 1968. He was survived by his wife, Florence and five children. Major Lohr was buried with honors at Arlington National Cemetery. He also received several other honors and citations for his accomplishments. In its obituary, the *Tribune* quoted Mayor Richard J. Daley, "There are few men who have made such great contributions to our city in so many ways. He gave many millions of visitors an appreciation of Chicago and millions of Chicago families wonderful opportunities for education and entertainment." And so I end my advocacy of the Lakefront Legacy of Lenox Lohr.

But, how do I explain his anonymity? Surely he must have been a humble man, satisfied with his accomplishments and unwilling to boast of their prodigious influence. Further, in contrast to those who used huge sums which they, in some cases, didn't earn themselves but used philanthropically to benefit future generations, Major Lohr did not have the wealth, political clout, or name recognition to be renowned for what he contributed by having something magnificent named for him. His reward is to remain unjustly obscure, but with a lakefront legacy second to none.

7

VANITY FAIR

The 1948 Chicago Railroad Fair was spectacular in every way. To begin with, it had an incomparable setting on the Chicago lakefront, a mile-long and fifty acres running from 20th-30th Streets with a heritage to match. It was roughly the same site as two other fabulous fairs, the granddaddy of them all, the World's Columbian Exhibition in 1893 and the legendary Century of Progress which between them represent half the stars on the Windy City's flag. The same grounds continue to attract millions of Chicago visitors as a piece of it holds the McCormick Place Exhibition complex. A fair siting indeed.

The concept of an extravagant fair featuring a single industry is a strange one to be sure. It makes more sense to learn the idea came from the Western Association of Railroad Executives which wanted to boost its business and boast of its achievements over the past century. Chicago was the natural place to hold such a fair since it had long been the dominant railroad city in the nation. Today, when there are only seven major railroads including a single passenger line, it's easier to understand their boldness if you know that in 1948 there were at least thirty-nine large railroads which pledged the necessary loans to fund the Fair. By the end of January, lines from the Atchison, Topeka & Santa Fe to the Wabash were on board. All they needed was organization.

Cover of the Chicago Railroad Fair *pageant program.*

The association established a board of directors made up mostly of railroad presidents. That could have led to jealousies, disputes, and disorganization, dooming the idea. If you factor in the insanely compact deadline of having a fair ready in 1948, and that it opened seamlessly and fully-realized on July 30 you know the board made the right choice of a general manager. As luck would have it, the exact man was right at hand, not so far from the grounds of the old fairs and already well known for his competence. More to the point, Major Lenox Lohr had been executive director of that Depression defying Century of Progress, then president of NBC and, since 1940, president of the Museum of Science and Industry.

To truly understand Major Lohr's achievement one needs to have a grasp of the Railroad Fair's scope. In six months, from scratch, a railroad access was built across Lake Shore Drive. Five miles of new track were laid for exploration and entertainment. In addition, more than two dozen major and as many minor structures were erected. Among the latter were a lakefront stage for a water-ski show, a merry-go-round with seats from passenger cars, tents for exhibitions by manufacturers of railroad equipment, an ice-skating rink, and three table-service restaurants including one in a modern dining car.

An essential element in the spectacle of the fair was the individual venues arranged by some of the lines, each highlighting the region they served. The official program states that the Chicago & Eastern Illinois had "Florida in Chicago" complete with a replica of Miami's beach (palm trees included), a colonial mansion, and the storied Bok Tower carillon. Not to be undone, the Illinois Central hosted ". . . a touch of New Orleans," a petite French Quarter complete with wrought iron balconies, music, and a lake-side patio for relaxation. The Burlington Lines, Great Northern, and Northern Pacific jointly sponsored a dude ranch and rodeo, not to mention a working model of Old Faithful and a Wild West town. The Rock Island Lines had a western dance show with continuous square dancing and teachers to instruct visitors.

The Santa Fe requested an Indian Village made to order with a Pueblo and other western Native American dwellings. "You (could) see Indians staging legendary dances, singing age-old Indian songs in strange Indian tongues." The program states the Chicago & Northwestern recreated the city's first railroad station which helped the visitor ". . . imagine unheralded Chicago of a century ago, a muddy frontier outpost . . ." Inside was a playhouse for live drama. It also displayed the restored *Pioneer*, Chicago's very first locomotive. The Union Pacific had prepared color films and other attractions from its eleven-state service area. The Denver and the Rio Grande offered a modern railroad coach outfitted as ". . . (a) studio-type motion picture theater." With no specific sponsor, the narrow-gauge Deadwood Central was ". . . a nostalgic throw-back to the West of years ago" which carried more passengers than any narrow-gauge in actual service.

As you can tell, the Fair was mostly western oriented, but nine eastern roads combined to exhibit an impressive 45-foot high sculpture of chromed steel rails with a revolving jeweled ball. A moving, talking 9-foot robot, "Genial Joe," interacted with visitors. Fair-goers could also view a dozen revolving dioramas and a library of giant picture books with self-turning pages.

There were offerings from big-name industry manufacturers as well. Chicago's own Pullman-Standard actually had two. The first was a Quonset style building which demonstrated the wide varieties of modern sleeping and lounge car accommodations. The second brought visitors behind the scenes of sleeping car construction and also showed the vital part the humble freight car played in an average American family's life. Railroad rivalries inspired exhibits, thus visitors could also view a Budd Company "Car of The Week," the latest in its own line of all stainless-steel streamline passenger cars including those with a rooftop observation deck, Budd's "Vista Dome."

Fully half of the five miles of track built for the Fair were filled by rolling stock—locomotives and cars representing the best of the most historic and modern the many railroads had to offer, ready for visitors to climb aboard and walk through. No ropes, no security guards, no "Look, but please don't touch" signs. Here, more securely shown, were legendary locomotives including The Tom Thumb, The Stourbridge Lion, DeWitt Clinton, and the record-setting 999 noted as ". . . a snorting behemoth of black steel and hot steam . . ." A car from the Lincoln funeral train and GM's Train of Tomorrow were also there. All told, hundreds of pieces of antique transportation rolling stock were gleaned from industry, commercial, museum, and private collections and wondrously all put in working order, an unprecedented achievement by itself which will never be duplicated.

And, if you still had time and energy for peripheral areas, you could visit some of the fifteen railroad supply and service firms which hopefully, ". . . add(ed) significantly to the dramatic impact of the national Railroad Fair." They ranged from the massive Unit Crane and Shovel Corp

". . . heavy duty crawler crane with magnet attachment to show . . . the loading and unloading of scrap steel," to the tiny, passive Encyclopedia Britannica display of historic railroad passes.

Perhaps what made the Railroad Fair so special is that while all of the above were well-done, instructive, and entertaining in their own right, they were akin to the sideshows to the Fair's signature feature, the "Wheels a-Rolling" pageant. Admission to the fairgrounds was a 1948 bargain of a quarter. The Fair guide and pageant program cost thirty-five cents. For an additional sixty cents, you saw a true extravaganza. The show was created by Edward Hungerford, who had written pageants for two earlier world's fairs. Did you notice the title of the pageant doesn't include a direct reference to railroads? That's because Hungerford's vision was to make the pageant a tribute to the varied history of all land travel in America. In fact, of twelve scenes, four featured no trains. Those non-railroad settings required fifty-six oxen and horses for pulling muscle powered transport and twenty antique motor vehicles. The other eight scenes were train-heavy with twenty-one locomotives or historic trains crossing the stage.

That stage itself was part of the spectacle. Facing a 5,000-seat grandstand, it was "ultra modern, 450 feet long and 100 feet deep." In between were two miles of multiple show tracks. The Fair program lists a small orchestra and chorus adding to the scenes with music adapted and directed by Isaac Van Grove. An original "Wheels a-Rolling Overture" was composed by Phillip and Helen Maxwell. The pageant required two narrators and a cast of 150 players to give life to all the rolling stock.

There is a side note that's appropriate to add here in some detail. It wasn't uncommon for celebrities to appear at the Fair and then sneak into bit parts of the pageant. What makes that especially important is that in 1948, one of those celebrities was Walt Disney, back in his home town. Donning a frock coat and stovepipe hat, he anonymously departed a 1890s train to be served a meal by a Harvey Girl. Walt had been persuaded to attend the Fair by his good friend and collaborator, Ward Kimball. Since both were also railroad buffs, they were allowed special license to operate some of the steam equipment. Surely they would have taken in all the exhibits in more ways than one. Within weeks of his visit, Disney was making preliminary plans for his dream theme park. Can it be only a coincidence that Disneyland included multiple narrow-gauge steam trains, a New Orleans Square, horse-drawn trolleys, turn-of-the-century vehicles, a carousel, a western frontierland, dancing Indians, a water ski show, audio-animatronics and so on, and that he decided to locate his bigger, better and newer theme park in balmy Florida? Rather, it is more likely that the legacy of the Chicago Railroad Fair is far more significant than old programs, photos, and fading memories.

Despite the frantic pace of preparation, the Fair not only opened on time but ran smoothly and was an immense critical and popular success. People came from great distances to see the Fair and pageant again and again. They could even commemorate their visit by sending a souvenir postcard from the grounds since the Fair had its own postmark and post office. It was so successful that its run was extended twice from its scheduled Labor Day closing. So successful, indeed, that it was held over for an expanded, equally popular 1949 season. And, so successful and efficiently run that despite the dismal record of great fairs losing money, Major Lohr, as he did with the Century of Progress, brought in a profit to repay investors.

The Chicago Railroad Fairs were unique in many ways. One of the most striking is that there never before was or will ever again be such a spectacular, certain, and ironic delineation of the high-water mark of such a dominant American industry. Even as they were celebrating their profound influence, the great American railroads were facing the factors which would take away both freight and passenger business.

We all learn that "Pride proceedeth a fall," so looking back from our perspective, a good way through the twenty-first century, knowing how quickly and far the great American railroad network would plummet, a logical first thought might be to question how the industry could have been so oblivious. There was surely complacency, but some other factors need to be considered as well. The infancy of the interstate highway system was even farther in the future than the election of President Eisenhower. So was the evolution of autos and trucks more suitable for long travels. As for air travel, the development of comfortable, fast, and reliable transcontinental passenger aircraft had been suspended during WWII. With the exception of the already inadequate DC-3, all long-range civilian aircraft were no more than dressed-up military planes. The Fairs showed that railroad technology was progressing. The replacement of dirty, inefficient steam locomotives with electric and diesel-electric was in full swing. Development of larger, lighter, stronger, and more comfortable passenger cars and advanced freight rolling stock was on track. Perhaps the most important factor, however, was that in 1948 most Americans hoped for, even expected, a recovery of vigorous economic prosperity. Nearly everyone assumed that recovery would be linked to the familiar and indispensable railroad network.

Yet within twenty short years the glory days of the American railroads were over. Public favor and government subsidies swung to the development and support of highway and air travel. The expanding interstates would increasingly connect the already auto-dependent cities. Ever larger and more efficient airports and aircraft would link places at speeds and in locations a train could never match. As it turned out, the decline of the railroad empire was inevitable, but its legacy is as certain as its demise. The two Chicago Railroad Fairs celebrated that legacy at the perfect time. We can only be amazed and grateful for them.

FROM PLEASURE TO TERROR

PART ONE—THE IROQUOIS THEATER FIRE

If the subject of the most tragic disasters in Chicago history should ever come up in conversation and some answer "The Great Chicago Fire of 1871" you can set them straight after reading these two stories. A person, even a native Chicagoan can be forgiven for thinking first of the Great Fire and in terms of width and breadth and property loss, it would be true. It burned uncontrolled for more than two full days and consumed hundreds of dilapidated wooden structures that would have taken years to eliminate by legal means. You can think of as "urban renewal" the hard way. That fire took 270 human lives and those of thousands of horses and cattle kept in those early days for milk and meat and just one reason Chicago was dismissed as a "cow town".

What rose on the devastated square miles of now empty lots were sturdy structures of brick, steel, and stone not only more fireproof but also more attractive for a city on its way up. 270 is a tragic number of deaths, but it's not by a long shot Chicago's deadliest disaster.

If you had visited Chicago in the early years of the twentieth century and were looking for an entertaining winter day you might think of taking the family to the city's newest and most opulent theater for a whimsical spoof of *Bluebeard*. Or if you were there in summer how about a day-long excursion on Lake Michigan? You'd be safe on any day unless you chose the wrong day. Then you and your family might die in a horrible fire or drown in the Chicago River trapped in a capsized cruise boat.

If you chose the Iroquois Theater on December 30, 1903, you and your children would be in mortal danger of being suffocated by acrid smoke and crushing bodies or to suffer the even worse fate of burning to death. In what could be accurately named a "perfect storm" of conditions combined to make the Iroquois Theater Fire not only the worst theater fire but still the worst single-building fire in American history.

The beginning was the building itself. Constructed at the reported cost of one million dollars in only a year, it was called by a critic in what would soon become *Variety* magazine ". . . the most beautiful . . . in Chicago and competent judges state that few theaters in America can rival its architectural perfections." This description was widely acclaimed, but it tragically disguised the fact that many safeguards had been ignored in the haste to finish the building. Many lapses were consciously caused by greed. Other hazards were common practices in theaters nationwide.

The Iroquois was declared ". . . fireproof beyond all doubt" by George Williams, Chicago Commissioner of Buildings and Ed Laughlin, its fire inspector. In fact, the building was far from it and the officials had been bribed Chicago style to approve it. Compare their glib assurances to the warnings in *Fireproof*, a leading journal whose editor William Clendenin noted the absence of sprinklers, fire alarms, or even a telephone. He also reported the absences of required fire-fighting devices, the illegal single staircase to the seats, and the excess of wood trim throughout the interior in his searing evaluation. Naturally, it was ignored.

Among the violations besides the ones mentioned by Clendenin was a fire escape in the alley which did not reach the ground and caused the deaths of more than a hundred. The required asbestos curtain separating the stage and seats was later be proven to be 90% cheap paper and it hadn't been checked to see if it would clear stage apparatus when dropped. Fire exits were unmarked, even covered by drapery to make them look like windows. The only fire apparatus purchased and available were named

Kilfyre extinguishers designed to spread a smothering powder at the base of the flames but totally useless when the flames were overhead.

Other deadly features were legal, accepted, and even standard in theaters. All entry doors opened inward and locked to prevent those without tickets from sneaking in. Similarly, accordion gates were closed and locked in the two balconies during performances to block anyone bold enough to try slipping up to a better seat in the darkened theater.

Final factors in the perfect storm were a combination of fateful timing and greed. It was near the end of the winter school holidays and it was a beautiful, cold day so it was very enticing for a mother to take her children to see the great theater and the highly rated family play featuring one of the most popular comics of the day, Eddie Foy. The manager of the theater was so anxious to have a full house after weeks of less than expected audiences that he sold standing room only tickets to more than two hundred patrons thus exceeding the theater's legal capacity. They crowded into the backs of the balconies and were even sitting in the aisles. After all, it was a brand new, highly acclaimed and fire-proof theater. What could go wrong?

According to surviving witnesses, including the backstage cast and crew which largely escaped, the thing that went wrong was a spotlight shorting out and beginning to burn. In turn, the fire spread to the fly loft filled with dozens of oily, flammable backdrops. The "fireproof" curtain had to be lowered by hand because the technician in charge of engaging the electrically-powered controls was sitting in the audience taking in the show. It would have probably made little difference because the curtain snagged on a cable which was designed to let a fairy "fly" out over the audience. As the fire spread so did the fear of the audience. Eddie Foy made sure his young son was taken to safety and then went on stage to shout for the audience to stay calm and orderly. He shouted to the orchestra to "Play an overture. Play anything for God's sake." To their credit, the musicians did stay to play but soon had to abandon the pit and flee backstage to be saved.

The fire actually smoldered for a time due to the lack of oxygen in the theater, but that ended fatally when first the stage door and then dual cargo doors were opened by escapees. A blast of freezing air was sucked in causing a back-draft fireball to explode into the auditorium. On the main floor, people had a better chance of survival because they had easy access to the wide staircase. Those in the balcony were not so fortunate. Not only did they come upon those locked gates which could be opened only by ushers, most of whom had fled for their own lives without unlocking the gates, they were trapped and smothered or burned to death in piles six feet high. Most of the dead were from the balconies where hundreds of corpses were found still sitting in their seats, instantly suffocated by the oxygen being drawn into the fireball, then burned beyond recognition.

In the lobby, the insatiable fire burned much of all that wooden trim and fabric while hundreds looked for ways out, including unmarked exits and locked exit doors which only opened inwards. A few of the doors were forced open. One lucky man in the audience happened to have an icebox key with him that opened another door. Many others were able to follow him to safety, but there were no more escapes similar to this one. Women and children were found by the dozens trapped in every doorway. The piles were so tightly packed that many people were suffocated. Miraculously, because the fire ran out of fuel relatively quickly, a precious few were protected from fumes and flames and lived for another day, never to forget the terror and loss and the guilt of surviving.

Many balcony patrons headed for the fire escape only to find themselves trapped twenty feet off the ground. As the flames approached many chose to jump rather than burn or were pushed over by those still alive inside. So many jumped that a few survived their falls broken by the pile of dead beneath them. Across the alley, some quick-thinking workmen were decorating an office. They were able to stretch a long ladder across the space to let a few more be saved. The old Iroquois Theater building is long gone but the alley still has a name and reputation as "Death Alley." It's always a stop on Haunted Chicago tours and some of those who are brave enough to use it report paranormal activity.

The fire department was only notified of the fire when a stage-hand arrived on foot as the nearest firehouse. An all-city alarm was immediately issued, but by the time they got to the Iroquois, the fire had almost completely burned itself out and could be fought. The real problem was the thick, acrid smoke which blinded the rescuers. The had to carefully enter the auditorium where they immediately began to find bodies—lots of bodies. As it was with the collapse of the World Trade Center almost a century later, it became apparent there were very, very few survivors left to find inside. The lucky few who did escape were already outside being tended by others or standing in stunned groups. It became quickly apparent that the work of the fire department was going to change from rescue to recovery. Incredibly, the fire had its deadly work in only fifteen minutes. The building was completely gutted.

As the air cleared, the true horror of the fire became apparent. The dead were carried out and at first stacked like firewood on the curb for later pick up. It is said a silent crowd of 50,000 came to see. To add to the ghastly scene, dozens of ghouls came to rob the dead.

That many corpses were too many to be taken to any one place nearby, so dozens of temporary morgues were volunteered. Freight wagons, express wagons, and Marshall Field delivery wagons were all volunteered for moving the bodies. Wherever they were taken they were laid out in long rows for identification by family members. Those who had been burned beyond recognition could only be identified by trinkets or jewelry that happened to have survived the corpse robbers. Slowly family members shuffled past the rows searching in one place or another until they found their loved ones. In some instances, a small body or two and a larger one was so fused they had to be laid out still intertwined. In those days before modern refrigeration, many of the worst were immediately buried in a mass grave in Graceland Cemetery to prevent contamination of the living. The next day was a day of funerals. There were not nearly enough hearses for the task so those wagons which had been volunteered the day before were used again.

When the death toll of a tragedy reaches over six hundred souls and in great numbers those of women and children who were supposed to be spared even the thought of such terrors there must be repercussions. Charges were brought against the theater's owner and manager. The manager was tried and convicted of malfeasance, and the owner of

Police officers guarding the dead at the Iroquois Theatre fire. (Courtesy of the Wikimedia Commons public domain.)

manslaughter. The bribed city officials were protected and not indicted. As time passed the public lost interest in punishment as it willfully buried the terrible memories of the fire and attorneys succeeded in getting the verdicts reversed. The only person to serve time was one of the small fry, a saloon owner who was robbing the dead, ironically even as bodies were being laid out in his establishment.

As often happens, improvement came at a great price. The terrible loss of life brought many improvements in theater design and fire protection to all theaters in America. The fire inspired an invention which enables doors to be locked but with an exit panic bar which opens doors without a key. The device was so ingenious that we still use it when we open a door from the inside in public buildings. All exit doors were ordered to open outwards and all gates to prevent moving from balcony to balcony were made illegal and removed. Fire alarms, telephones, and approved fire-fighting devices were made mandatory. Sprinkler systems were required to be retrofitted in existing theaters and built into new ones. Fire escapes were placed under much greater scrutiny. All of this is so standard today it is seldom considered and especially at what price it came, but it was a different time and many lessons have to be learned the hard way.

The Iroquois was rebuilt using the original surviving walls but it didn't last long. It was shunned. Eventually, it was torn down to the foundation and a completely new theater was built at the same address but saving the iconic facade. The new theater was named the Oriental and became one of Chicago's downtown movie palaces. Today it is still a popular performance stage theater with the name "Ford Center for the Performing Arts."

The deadly Iroquois Theater fire never did capture the imagination or stature of the Great Chicago Fire though it took twice the number of lives. There was no Mrs. O'Leary, no lantern, no cow to fire the imagination. The Great Fire burned for two days and the flames could be seen for a dozen miles. It was covered by papers across the nation as it happened. And though deadly, by far most of those in its path had a chance to escape.

No one can find the Iroquois fire anything but a horrible and preventable loss of innocent lives. It was too much for people to wrap their minds around, as we would say today, so easier to forget as it has been.

FROM PLEASURE TO TERROR

PART TWO—THE SINKING OF THE SS EASTLAND

It's easy to find ways that the Iroquois Theater Fire and the capsizing of the SS *Eastland* are opposite. Death by suffocation, trampling, crushing falls, or burning as opposed to drowning.—death by fire or death by water. But considered carefully, there are more ways in which they become similar. Most obvious is that they both caused massive death tolls and boundless sorrow for others. Both came from the greed of engineers and owners. Both were at least partially caused by bad design and cutting corners on safety. The casualties in both resulted at least in part from overcrowding. Tragically both began as enjoyable adventures for families. Finally, both disasters which deserve to be better remembered are almost completely forgotten today, their locations marked only by bronze plaques.

The SS *Eastland* was built as an excursion ship in 1902 and immediately dubbed "The Speed Queen of the Great Lakes." As with most similar boats plying the inland sea with few deep-water harbors, she was built without a keel to reduce draft for shallow water. Stability was supposed to be controlled by means of water-filled ballast tanks. The contemporary engineering called for powerful pumps to switch the weight of the water from port to starboard to maintain "an even keel." (The lake boats were all round-bottomed and thus had no actual keel.) Most of these boats were top-heavy by nature, especially the SS *Eastland*. No test had been made with the ship underway and loaded with passengers for it wasn't required at the time. In addition, the boat which had been licensed to carry five hundred passengers was now regularly carrying up to two thousand as it passed from owner to owner.

It had trouble from the start. In 1904 it nearly capsized in the open lake with the already bloated passenger load increased to 2,500. A similar incident occurred when the *Eastland* was overloaded in 1906. Neither incident was reported because it had passed all the testing that was required.

It was also fitted out to meet new regulations which came as a result of lessons learned in the HMS *Titanic* disaster just three years earlier. All ships or boats the size of the *Eastland* at 275 feet had to be equipped with lifeboat capacity and life jackets for all on board. The lifeboats alone weighed hundreds of pounds each and the 2500 life vests were over fifty pounds thus significantly increasing the instability of the boat. It seems beyond ironic that new safety rules to prevent loss of life added to it.

On the fateful morning of July 24, 1915, the *Eastland* was one of five excursion boats chartered by the sprawling Western Electric Co, maker of most of the telephone equipment used in the country. It employed thousands of immigrants, many of them Czechs who sometimes were expected to work seven days a week. So, having a Sunday off was a rare treat though it was tempered somewhat by a Western Electric directive that gave two choices to its employees, either attend the excursion or work. The excursion included a thirty-eight-mile cruise across Lake Michigan to a company picnic in Michigan City, Indiana, and back.

By 7:00 A.M. the boats were nearly full. A few stragglers came almost too late and one had to jump across the gap between ship and shore after the loading ramps had been removed. Almost immediately the *Eastland* began a list to port, away from the dock. Quickly though she was righted, calming the passengers, many of whom had paused before heading below decks with their families to find room to spend the pleasant day. Hundreds of others remained on the top decks to witness the beginning of the voyage.

At 7:23, the *Eastland* listed even more to port until water began to flood the ship through open gangways and portholes. The crew's attempt to control the roll was either badly handled or the ballast system inadequate for the situation because the roll continued until the *Eastland* had come to rest on its side in twenty feet of water. It was quick and deadly turning from 45 degrees to 90 degrees in just two minutes. From beginning to end the *Eastland* sank in just fifteen minutes, about the same time as it took the Iroquois Theater Fire to take 602 lives.

Crew members fled to the top deck leaving hundreds of others below to their fates. In actual fact, there was little they could have done to help. Those on the top deck were catapulted into the river fully clothed and not one with a life jacket. When the disaster was first spotted several smaller boats in the river came to pick survivors out of the water, but that was about all the rescuing there was to do. As with the Iroquois fire, the rescue became a recovery. If the theater fire took a disproportionate toll of women and children, the *Eastland* sinking took entire families, twenty-one of them to be exact. The average age of the dead was later reckoned at just twenty-four. There were few injuries among the survivors so most of them were sent home in private cars in which not one

The capsized Eastland *and vessels assisting to remove the dead. (Courtesy of the Wikimedia Commons public domain.)*

driver protested. As the bodies were recovered sometimes a stretcher was laden with two little forms. In all, over 800 people died that day that began with so much anticipation. Again spectators saw bodies stacked like cord wood.

The sheer number of corpses was again a problem. This time however there was a building large enough to handle all of them. Trucks and wagons from many sources were filled with bodies and taken to the Second Regiment Armory on the drill floor. There was only one place to go to identify the dead and the sad task was made easier because all the victims were recognizable. Some may have felt special grief for the bodies still looked as if they could stand up and leave.

The corpses were neatly laid out in rows of eighty-nine and that tragic shuffling of feet for those looking for loved ones was again heard. Because identification was so much easier searchers were limited to only twenty minutes to look. Within the day all the victims had been claimed except for one little boy who was nicknamed "Little Feller" by a sympathetic press. He didn't have long to wait for soon a girl recognized him as a neighborhood playmate.

The next day was another day of funerals when the delivery of the dead was made possible only by means of trucks and wagons volunteered by Chicago citizens. In cemeteries all across the Chicago area as many as fifty-two grave diggers working twenty-four hours a day couldn't keep up so there were some mass burials. The largest number of burials reflected the burden of loss that fell on the Czech community as 170 bodies were taken to Bohemian National Cemetery.

A fair question is why such a terrible tragedy is today largely forgotten. There are some logical explanations, certainly more so than in the selective forgetting of the Iroquois Fire. Unlike the *Titanic* sinking the passengers on the *Eastland* included no one other than working class and most immigrants at that. No rich, no famous, no one whom the world needed to remember. Because it was over in mere minutes there were no legends of "women before children" or couples willing to die together or bands playing "Nearer My God to Thee" as the boat went down. As the survivors of the *Titanic* were brought to New York there

Entrance to the Bohemian National Cemetery. (Photo obtained from Wikimedia Commons, courtesy of https://www.flickr.com Zol87.)

were news stories lasting weeks but not for the *Eastland*. You can even add the fact that it did not even sink but feebly laid over on its side as if resting (The *Eastland* was later re-floated, rechristened *Wolverine* and saw WWII service as a training vessel.) In addition, another great liner, the H MS *Lusitania* had been sunk by a German submarine in May and would be headline news for weeks because it represented a sea change in the rules of war and many of the victims were American citizens.

There are only one of those ominous plaques along the River Walk to mark the place now, but you'll find it in a pleasant, terraced amphitheater on the south bank of the river which has become a favorite of downtown employees enjoying a sunny luncheon.

10

CHICAGO IN THE AIR

A TALE OF THREE AIRPORTS

"Forward-thinking" isn't a term you would associate with politicians. Risk makes them nervous and change makes them want to dig in their heels, but it isn't always that way. If there is one thing the City Fathers of Chicago had learned from history it was the importance of being in the center of a transportation network. Sailing ships and railroads had made the city and the fortunes of many of its most influential civic leaders.

It wasn't a certainty but not surprising when aviation was beyond its infancy and entering its adolescence that the most long-sighted Chicago leaders could see a time when air transport of passengers and goods would develop. By the nineteen-teens, there were already a few grassy airports around the city. Grant Park on the lakefront had an Air Park and though it was used more for regular dirigible operations, it was large enough for the primitive bi-planes or "aereoplanes" that many young men had learned to love during WWI. That is until a disaster occurred that was so incredible it might have come from the pages of Steam Punk fiction. A dirigible which was flying to the White City Amusement Park lost control and by terrible misfortune crashed as precisely through the glass atrium roof dome of the Illinois Trust and Savings Bank Building as if it were aimed. On the floor of the bank, dozens of clerks and tellers were trapped by an explosive cascade of burning fuel and hydrogen. Twelve were burned or crushed to death. Operations at Grant Air Park were immediately ordered ended, but that didn't slow the flying. The activities were transferred to Checkerboard Airport outside the city limits, surrounded by farms.

America's brief experience with WWI aviation had created almost no attention as a useful weapon by the military. As the nation returned to a disillusioned Isolationism, the Army and Navy returned to what they knew best, infantry and cavalry or battleships. If there was to be a future in flying, it was going to be civilians who saw to it. Young aviators lead the way. The "daring young men in their flying machines" were hooked. They couldn't give it up so they invented a way to almost learn a living (or dying) doing it. Many of them bought surplus JN4s nicknamed "Jennies" or "Flying Coffins" and spread over the country barnstorming. They'd fly over a rural community where literally no one had seen an airplane before. A crowd would gather and the pilot would earn just enough for fuel and repairs by giving rides and lessons. If he were lucky, he might be invited to stay with a local family. Pilots were not only nomadic, they also were exotic and considered quite romantic as well. The Barnstormers did more than entertain the folks from a thousand tiny towns; they spread the interest and knowledge of aviation in the best way possible—in person. One of the first of the Barnstormers was the legendary Bessie Coleman, an African-American woman who had to learn to fly in France. Bessie's home base was at Checkerboard Field. If you've rented a car at O'Hare recently, you've been on Bessie Coleman Drive.

The federal government relied on the railroads for 99 percent of mail transfers but believed there was a future in flying the mail and making a profit. Air mail routes were planned and pilots hired including a very young man with the immortal name of Charles Augustus Lindbergh. Flying the mail was the ultimate in risk and challenge for early pilots, many of whom died in crashes. Aircraft were primitive, having no instruments unless it was a compass. There were no air maps so pilots relied on road maps which they kept folded under their laps to keep them from blowing out of the open cockpit, embodying the term "flying by the seat of my pants."

As early as 1922, Chicago had an Aeronautical Bureau which saw enough promise in the future of civil aviation that it dedicated a square mile of land at 63rd Street and Cicero Ave as an airfield and named it "Municipal Airplane Landing Field" used primarily for practice landings for the successor to Checkerboard Field, Maywood Park. It is the exact location of Midway today.

Three years later not only was air mail flying out of the new field but limited charter passenger service had been established. The name of the field was changed to the shorter and more appropriate "Chicago Municipal Airport." William Boeing brought his passenger airline to Municipal where he merged his air service with others to form United Air Lines.

If this story is about anything beyond the history of Chicago's airports, it is also about how their progress went hand-in-glove with the development of commercial aviation. In May of 1928, the newly named field was dedicated and its business quickly soared. Ground traffic now required a flagman to direct planes to the expanding number of runways and taxiways. The runways were paved with gravel to permit larger and heavier aircraft like the Ford Trimotor to land. There were more hangars, shops, better night-time lighting to extend operations hours, and ramps for boarding. A small passenger terminal was built for fliers' comfort. The additions paid dividends. By 1931 Municipal has earned its title as "The World's Busiest Airport," one it would keep for three-and-a-half decades.

In the same decade as city aviation, officials were doubling the area of Municipal's acreage. They were seeing a future when the "neighborhood airport" reputation that had helped it grow would limit its capacity to be expanded. By the mid-30s, earlier commercial airplanes were replaced by newer, faster, heavier "airliners." The best by far was the Douglas DC-3, but the Boeing 247 was close and there were various Lockheed, Martin, and other variants. For more usable space, the city went to court to over-turn a grant that gave a "perpetual lease" to the Chicago and Western Indiana Railroad, or "Belt Line," a route across a great deal of the airfield.

The city won the battle and the tracks were moved west. This was the final expansion for Chicago Municipal.

When you're at your prime in popularity and profit it's sometimes easy to dismiss foreboding decisions made elsewhere. One of the clearest was the government's decision to purchase a huge parcel of rural land surrounding a small railroad stop named Orchard Place with the idea of someday building a new and massive airport there. The decision was purely based on the fact that Municipal could grow no more and if the city wasn't forward thinking again it would be left with only one airport and another reason to be called The Second City.

The beginning of WWII greatly increased the critical need for development of the new airport facility, so a regional meeting convinced the Army Air Corp to build an enormous assembly plant at the new "Orchard Place Field." Douglas, for years the leader in commercial aircraft development, was granted a contract to build the Army's largest transport aircraft—the four-engined C54 Skymaster.

The main assembly plant at Douglas was built of wood because of wartime shortages and became the largest wooden structure in the world covering two million square feet. The construction was supervised by The Army Corp of Engineers using a workforce of 8,500. When the war was over, so was the Douglas contract for Skymaster assembly. Douglas was less than enchanted with the terrible maintenance problems caused by the assembly building. It had no wish to continue to build aircraft in the harsh climate of Northern Illinois so it was quick to move its operation to Southern California. That left one now unnecessary building but many useful supporting structures. There were acres and acres of already paved taxiways and runways. There were ramps capable of the take-offs, landings, and maintenance of the heaviest airplanes. And even more acres of parking lots with enough for 3000 cars ready to use as well.

If Douglas didn't want the old plant, the Air Force didn't either so it was designated as surplus. The city stepped forward to offer to take over the former Douglas Field. After negotiations, the federal government got the huge tract off its expense lists and the city of Chicago had an immense new property for no cost. Work on a second airport began immediately.

By the fall of 1955, it was ready to open for limited operations. One of the first duties of the newly elected Mayor Richard J. Daley was to attend the dedication of the new airfield.

Except for its former residents potentially, no one was fond of the name Orchard Place. It sounded too much like one of the new shopping malls that were springing up all over the metropolitan area. A more appropriate and dignified name was sought. Happily, there was a perfect choice which no one had any trouble accepting. Edward "Butch" O'Hare was from Chicago and a naval aviator who had shot down an entire flight of seven Japanese bombers to defend his carrier, earning a Medal of Honor for his achievement. He had died later in the war so there would be no later-life problems to tarnish the name. And, maybe best of all, he was Irish. That got the mayor on board. Hizzoner was famed for his frequent malapropisms, one of the most endearing being when he often called his new airport "O'Hara." Butch is recognized in a large and striking display with an authentic F4F Wildcat fighter. It was the earlier version of the much larger, heavier F6F Hellcat he was flying on the fateful day, so it is entirely proper that it be shown in a position of landing on a carrier deck. The name of the original airport, Orchard Place Field, lives on in O'Hare's international airport designation ORD.

Chicago Municipal had the common thought to choose a more identifiable name. Similar to O'Hare it chose a well-known name from WWII—"Midway"—to honor the victory that many consider the turning point of the war. In that epic battle, all the combat was aerial so it fit with the idea of aviation. Many first-time travelers at Midway are surprised to see a real WWII navy "war-bird" suspended from the ceiling in Terminal A. The plane on display is a Douglas SBD "Dauntless." The Dauntlasses carried the fight to the enemy at The Battle of Midway at the cost of great casualties of the aircraft and two-man crews. This one has a great story behind it. During the war, thousands of navy pilots were trained at Glenview Naval Air Station near Chicago on makeshift aircraft carriers converted from old lake steamers. The student pilots were notorious for splashing their planes in the lake but the water on the floor of Lake Michigan is too cold for any vegetation to survive so some of the

A F4F Grmman Wildcat at O'Hare Airport - tribute to Edward "Butch" O'Hare. (Courtesy of the Wikimedia Commons public domain.)

old planes are still in decent shape. This is one of them. It was located by divers and delicately raised by a salvage crew. Next, it was completely refurbished on the outside and given this place at Midway. Midway has a double meaning, of course, as it denotes the location of the busy in-town airport halfway across America.

Meigs Field had begun its short life only a couple of years before fulfilling another of Mayor Daley's priorities, having an airport close enough to Downtown to be easily accessible by business executives and wealthy amateur pilots. Named for Merill Meigs who oversaw its establishment, Meigs always was a compromise between location and size. It had room for only one short runway, but it was within ten minutes of downtown.

Meigs may have been a favorite of Mayor Daley I, but it was definitely a thorn in the side of his son, Mayor Daley II who wanted to have the land for a nature park. Before his petition for ending the FAA certification of Meigs had been granted, he ran out of patience and took things into his own hands. In 2003 he ordered a mid-night raid on the Meigs runway. Bulldozers cut a series of deep "X's" across the pavement, ruining it and making it impossible to use Meigs Field again.

Earlier in this chapter, it was noted that the future of Chicago's first airport was inescapably linked to that of commercial aviation. Both needed to be able to progress in a balancing act. For twenty-five years, the balance worked. When there was a leap forward in air travel and aircraft technology, Midway was able to bound ahead to match it. In 1958, that balance failed because the leap of technology was too great to be matched by Midway, so the era of the jet airliner began with the first flights of the pioneering Boeing 707. The Jet Age had begun.

The 707 and the DC8 were both far too fast, too heavy, and required longer runways than the neighborhood locked Midway could provide. As jet aircraft advanced the newer models were nearly all bigger, heavier, and carried more passengers. These aircraft were capable of flying non-stop routes from Chicago to five continents so O'Hare became that much more important. It had plenty of room to add runways and taxiways, build larger terminals with more gates, and improved luggage handling capability. Even the enclosed "Jetways" that are taken for granted to keep us out of the elements started at O'Hare.

Carriers began to move operations from Midway to O'Hare. In 1961, O'Hare stripped Midway of the proud distinction it held for thirty-five years as "World's Busiest Airport." By the mid-seventies, Midway had been effectively abandoned by all carriers. They could not stay competitive operating simultaneously out of two airports. The grass wasn't exactly growing in the runways yet but it was close. Operation of shuttle, private, and executive aviation did increase because the skies were now empty and there were few delays in landings or take offs. The runways were long enough for executive jet aircraft and there were empty hangars and maintenance facilities. The FAA kept Midway open so it did have up-to-date ground control. Years before the Stevenson Expressway (I-55) had been built. Using it, Midway was also closer in time and distance to Downtown than O'Hare. Still, there was serious discussion about selling the land to developers.

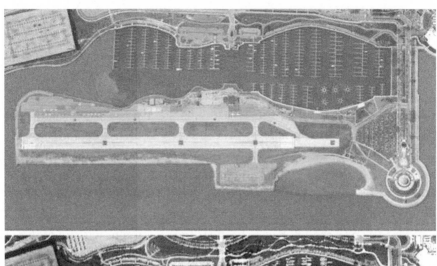

Meigs Field then and now.

Mayor Daley was acutely aware of Midway's fate for it's practically in his neighborhood. He was South Side born and raised so he had a true affinity for it. He twisted a few arms to get a couple of carriers to return to Midway operations. But it was a charade which fooled no one. The attempt failed. Deserted Midway still had thousands of "fans" who were heartbroken at its ignominious fall. They were people who remembered the days when the airport was a destination by itself. Families would arrive and climb to the observation deck to see who could identify the most aircraft designs correctly. They might explore the terminal and even have a meal at the Marshall Field Clouds Room before walking or driving home.

Neighborhood boys were attracted to the hangars where they would make friends with pilots and mechanics who might become their mentors. More than a few found their career path starting at Midway. Both boys and girls would stand at the perimeter fence in line with a runway to experience the thrilling ground-shaking sound of four huge piston engines operating at full power as the DC6s and DC7s flew less than fifty feet over their heads.

One man has a memory that has stayed with him for the rest of his life. Here are the words of Pat Bukiri: "When I was a little kid the planes were coming so low my father would say 'Duck, duck! Here they come!' I'd be laying on the seat as the plane came roaring over. 'Oh man, now I have to clean the roof of my car! The planes keep leaving wheel marks on the roof.' When I got home, of course, I actually climbed on top of the car because I wanted to see the wheel marks."

Would any of those with fond Midway memories have been willing to bet on its recovery? Who would set the odds? Would 100 to 1 or even 1000 to 1 against recovery be taken? Midway's emptiness seemed so complete that only a minor miracle could save it from the wrecker's ball and jackhammers. As we know, miracles are often brought by angels with wings. Midway's miracle came with wings too when the small, upstart Southwest Airlines came flying out of the West.

Southwest began as a regional carrier flying only within the huge state of Texas. In a series of expansions, it came to the Midwestern market and Midway. There it found a perfect niche to fill. The big airlines were operating out of O'Hare and had seemingly lost focus on the domestic market to a great degree, emphasizing jumbo jets to take people around the world. They spent hundreds of millions to create convenient new terminals, gates, walkways, airport services, and parking. The O'Hare Hilton Hotel was erected on airport property and rental car services were made more efficient. The "giants" all had their eyes on the big skies.

Southwest saw the underserved business of flying within the forty-eight states. They looked at every major city and often found a market and open gates. These days the skies over Midway or Orlando or Denver are filled with the distinctively decorated orange and blue paint jobs on each of Southwest's fleet of over seven hundred 737-500 planes. They are impressive for even at a distance they are identifiable as sort of flying billboards. The Southwest model extends to baggage (two bags each fly free), onboard personnel (relaxed and funny), and large numbers of flights to smaller cities at bargain prices. Follow it and you will improve the bottom line by flying more planes with full passenger capacity. It's fun to imagine Southwest choosing a company theme song. They might well consider "Let's Get Away from It All" a hit by Frank Sinatra, "We'll travel 'round from town to town. We'll visit every state. I'll repeat, I love you sweet in all the forty-eight."

The phenomenal success story wasn't unnoticed by larger airlines. It would have been impossible to miss. They began to return to Midway with flights within the continental United States. It was a risky investment for Midway had fallen from grace for the very reason that airlines could not operate out of both O'Hare and Midway competitively. Was it even possible there would be enough demand for air travel that once again Chicago could have two successful first-class airports? It surely wasn't the only reason, but Boeing brought out a so-called STOL (Short Take-off and Landing) jet, the 757. Larger than its 737s or 727s, it can fly faster, farther, and with more passengers aboard, yet still land and take-off from Midway. Its sight there is now common.

Mayor Richard J. Daley had died suddenly in 1976 when Midway was at its lowest point. His son Mayor Richard M. Daley remembered his father's affinity for Midway and saw a business opportunity that needed help. As more airlines returned, he oversaw a $700,000,000 renovation of every aspect and service an airport can provide. A brand-new terminal with reconfigured gates, a food court and friendly bars, useful and interesting shops, and services were included. A brand-new, second-to-none baggage delivery system was designed and installed to get passengers on their way right away.

Outside, Midway wasn't neglected. The entrance and exits from Cicero Ave. were reconfigured. Cicero Ave. was increased to eight lanes from Midway to I-55. The CTA brought rapid transit to and from downtown on its new Orange Line. New decks for both short-term

A WWII aircraft in Midway Airport. This is a Douglas SBD "Dauntless."

and long-term parking were built and rental car shuttles and agencies improved. Traffic control for private cars, taxis, and limousines made them all flow more freely. All of this would have been badly-spent money if upgrades weren't also made in computer-controlled ground control to get off as many fights on-time as possible. It all worked together to successfully increase Midway passenger flow. Today it sends off and welcomes about one million flights annually.

If you've ever traveled off the interstate system in rural America east of the Rockies, you will have seen small churches and their attendant churchyards. In many cases, the congregation has gone away and only the dead are left. It's not surprising then that if you take over 5000 acres of farmland you will also have some of these churches and cemeteries. The acres of O'Hare did have three. Each was left in peace until expansion caused the need for the land. At the foot of runway 9-R, you once could have found St. Johannes Evangelical Lutheran Cemetery. When yet another runway (10-C) was needed, the cemetery was taken and 1400 bodies disinterred and reburied in other cemeteries scattered throughout the area. A second, less well-known cemetery was Wilmer's Old Settlers Cemetery. It had originally been an Indian burial ground. Again, all bodies were exhumed and moved to other cemeteries.

There's a frightening truth in air travel. The more flights that are handled at an airport the greater the chances of crashes become. The number has shrunk to only a handful in the past sixty years. In 1955, a Braniff pilot brought his plane in too low, clipped a fifteen foot gas station sign and pancaked onto the street. Its forward movement caused it to skid through the perimeter fence, flip over, and break up. Miraculously there was no fire so the twenty-one survivors had a chance to be rescued. Twenty-two others died in the crash.

The Braniff crash was an exception to the certainty that if a plane comes down outside the field, people on the ground will die. That's happened twice. In 1959, a TWA Super Constellation carrying cargo fell from the sky and crashed through a neighborhood. An inferno followed powered by aviation fuel and burning homes. More people on the ground were killed than on the plane: nine residents and a three-man flight crew. That definitely wasn't the case thirteen years later when a United Airlines DC7 crashed in the neighborhood killing all on board and two on the ground.

It should be noted that these crashes were caused by piston-engine aircraft. In order to be powerful, a piston engine must be made extremely complex with literally tens of thousands of parts which must all work. There are a lot more things that can go wrong with a piston engine than a jet engine, which is much simpler. Once jets and turboprops became the standard at Midway, the air crashes fell to zero. Now there were no disasters, just the skids and overruns that a small airport like Midway has to offer. The worst overrun came on a snowy night when a plane skidded on the icy runways through the perimeter fence and collided with a car, sadly killing a young girl.

At O'Hare there have been two fatal crashes involving jets. The earlier of the two was a collision between a plane landing and another taxiing to take off. A ground controller had inadvertently assigned both planes the same runway. The outgoing jet tried to pull up to avoid a collision but couldn't. It tore the entire tail assembly off the plane on the ground then crashed, killing nine.

O'Hare was the scene of the most horrific air crash before 9/11 and still holds the grisly record of being the worst single-aircraft disaster in American history. American Flight 191, a Lockheed 1011 made a normal take-off run. Just as it started rotation from the ground, observers on the ground and in the tower saw an incredible, terrifying sight. The entire left (port) engine pod had torn from the wing and crashed to the ground. It is a fact that nearly all multi-engines jets can fly, even land, with one engine dead. In this situation, it was more than only a dead engine. The jumbo jet had to have the power of both engines to take off. In addition, because the engine pod was under the wing, none of the flight crew knew what had happened. And, if this situation wasn't bad enough, it got worse. The port engine is the one with the connections from an onboard generator which powered all the electronic instrumentation in the cockpit. The giant aircraft made a slow bank to port and crashed to the ground causing a giant fireball and instantly killing all 258 people on board. Because it happened at O'Hare where no houses surround it on every side, the crash took only two lives on the ground. Ironically, the vacant field where 191 crashed and burned was a defunct small airport.

This is the story of three of America's great airports. One which grew only to be destroyed in an act of vandalism, another which just grew and grew, and a third which rose and fell only to be re-born. Meigs Field, O'Hare Airport, and Midway have varied and interesting histories. They all three had a role in fulfilling the vision the Aviation Bureau had way back in 1922 to make Chicago the Crossroads of America in the Air.

11

THE SHOW IS OVER

CHICAGO NEIGHBORHOOD MOVIE PALACES

For Gen X, Millennials, and pretty much anyone born after 1970, the three words *neighborhood movie palace* will draw a blank or, at best, a curious stare. When everyone goes to a film today, they virtually all must find and drive to a multiplex where they watch a wonderful film, but in a blank box without decoration or style. These venues are so homogeneous that from inside you could be watching in ten thousand different places and not be able to tell where you were.

But it wasn't always that way, especially in Chicago. If you were in one of Chicago's neighborhood movie palaces you would know instantly if you were in the Regal, the Uptown, the Patio, or any other of hundreds of the type.

Chicago was, after all, the pioneer in not only the neighborhood movie "theater" but the neighborhood movie palace. There was a great gulf between a movie theater and a movie palace. Size was important. A large movie theater would have seats for 500 to 800. Purpose was another difference. Movie theaters were only for showing films. But the most obvious way to distinguish theaters from palaces was style. Movie theaters were nice and usually clean but plain inside and outside. You could confuse one with another. Movie palaces, on the other hand, were nearly all huge, with a seating capacity between 800 to over 4,000. Movie palaces were full performance showplaces. Far from being just a place to show a movie they had large stages capable of the presentation of full Big Bands, stage shows, and dramatic performances. There was always a proscenium arch and a heavy ornate curtain. They all had a large auditorium and most had a balcony. Each had a loft for storage of backdrops and rooms for props and other equipment. There would be dressing rooms and rehearsal rooms. Full stage lighting was a necessity. All would have an orchestra pit and a sumptuously lighted multi-console organ with many pipes. The organ would often have the capability of being raised from the pit. In addition, the palaces would often be the anchor for apartments, shops, and other businesses including a hotel and even a bowling alley and billiard room in the same complex.

Style was supreme in neighborhood movie palaces and no expense was spared in making the interiors ornate, elegant, opulent, and ostentatious. In other words, unique and unforgettable. Good taste and restraint were not guidelines found in the movie palace architects' and designers' handbooks. Collectively the ethos of these manuals might be "Less is Less." Architectural styles were mixed and mashed for spectacular entries and auditoriums. Exteriors boasted broad canopy marquees illuminated by hundreds of colored lights and the name of the film, stars, and the stage show performers appearing all in large letters on a bright white background. Often there was a second vertical marquee rising up to four stories high that could be seen for blocks.

By the dawn of silent films, every large city in America from coast-to-coast had downtown movie palaces. They were all pretty much all spectacular in style and size, but they were also expensive to attend and it took a long time to get to them, putting them outside the reach of average people.

Chicago as an origin of the neighborhood movie palace concept was due to certain factors. One was population density. Each neighborhood contained thousands of apartments and a multiplicity of small homes that crowded each block on restrictive and narrow 33' wide lots. Chicago had the most extensive streetcar system in America, so if a movie palace was too far to reach on foot or you wanted to attend one in another neighborhood, it was often just a quick nickel trolley ride away. There were few private autos and no expressways to take you far away. Residents closely identified with their neighborhood's familiar schools, churches, banks, shops and stores, taverns and restaurants, organizations, and celebrations. The streets were quiet and safe and in some neighborhoods, ethnic cohesion was another comfort.

Residents felt they had everything they needed in the neighborhood and attending nearby theaters was another comfort. Downtown movie palaces seemed far away in both distance and culture. If they could have their own neighborhood movie palace, then so much the better. They would support it.

Movie palaces were mostly built during an age of two entertainment rivals. The older of the two was vaudeville. Every conceivable kind of act which could appear on stage did appear. The newcomer was the motion picture. Virtually all the neighborhood palaces were built before the age of sound and color movies. Silent films were of course very limited by comparison. They were always black and white. Printed frames had to be spliced into the film to explain a situation or location to the audience. Actors had to overemphasize facial expressions and body language to express emotion.

Vaudeville with its mixture of everything from stand-up comics to actual dog and pony shows were immediate, full of sound and color, and had an ever-changing variety of (mostly) funny and enjoyable acts. Movie palaces had the ability and usually did combine the two for one admission. Between showings of a film, the acts would come on. Here the film had an advantage. It was exactly the same at each screening and it never got tired. The performers would have to do as many as five or six shows a day and still be fresh. Their auditoriums were also leased for traveling shows, repertory dramas and comedies, concerts, pageants, religious services, and other functions.

Movie palaces were built with close cooperation between architect/designers and construction firms. They had to be well-financed as the cost was always measured in hundreds of thousands of dollars. The largest theater chain in the nation, Balaban & Katz, built many in the neighborhoods. Others were financed by local investors. Sometimes they were only a block or two away from each other, but all made a profit during the good times. Chicago has seventy-seven designated neighborhoods, but there were hundreds of movie palaces in them or the nearby suburbs.

Considering their location and significantly lower admission prices, it might stand to reason that the neighborhood palaces showed second run films. However, this was untrue. They showed the same films as the downtown theaters. Some of this could be made up by excellent sales at the concession stands. (A dime for popcorn and a fountain drink, anyone?) Also, their convenient locations packed the houses more often than the big theaters downtown.

Vaudeville ultimately waned in the face of competition from radio, sound movies, and technicolor movie palaces filled the seats with other enticements. Patrons looked for double features, sneak previews, short features, newsreels, and usually a first run cartoon from Disney, Warner Bros., or Walter Lantz. Many began the practice of showing advertisements for businesses with the previews. Saturday matinees were given over to children's shows, usually "B" westerns, cartoons, and cliff-hanger serials.

As the radio and the Great Depression kept more and more customers away, theaters of all sorts invented gimmicks to bring people in. One of the most prevalent and popular was "dish night." Anyone paying a full adult admission was handed a piece of crockery or flatware. Many a family collected completes sets of each. Some of these giveaways are now highly sought by collectors. "Jackpot" giveaways were also used. In these, one lucky ticket holder was awarded a percentage of the admission take for the performance.

Some neighborhood palaces succumbed to bankruptcy during the Depression. Others squeaked through and again thrived during WWII, especially because Chicago was a military town. Not only did it have many training and defense facilities, there were also millions of soldiers and sailors that passed through on trains.

What they could not successfully fight was television. The thousands who previously traveled to the palaces for enjoyment and entertainment could stay at home to laugh and gasp during the Golden Age of Television in the comfort of their own homes. The TV was almost free and families could supply their own refreshments and even liquor if desired.

From their construction, movie palaces were always threatened by costs of operation as large as their size. Maintenance, housekeeping, and repair personnel were usually union and costly in dollars and effectiveness. Ushers, ticket sellers and takers, hat check girls, projectionists, managers and their assistants, and even lounge attendants had to be not only paid but dressed in uniforms or formal wear as well. This enormous overhead doomed movie palaces when attendance dwindled.

A few were able to re-invent themselves as performance venues, featuring nearly every top name act in the country. Others were converted to art film, or "Indie" houses. A few became performing arts centers where everything from touring Broadway companies to ballet could perform.

Most went out of business though. They were much mourned, but salvageable. Some have been converted to other uses such as a CVS pharmacy, a McDonald's restaurant, and other retail establishments or parking lots. A few still stand in an uncertain state as loyal groups try to raise the tremendous sums needed to restore them. The great majority are gone completely, fallen to the wreckers. The only things left from these once magnificent structures are records, photos, and the fond memories of increasingly older Chicagoans.

It's impossible to appreciate the Chicago neighborhood movie palaces only from the written word, but let the following descriptions serve to help imagine what the city was like when they were still here. The Uptown theater is a good example of the neighborhood movie palace and is located at 4816 N. Broadway. It is one that once belonged to the Balaban and Katz chain. It was designed by the firm of Rapp and Rapp who designed other B & K theaters. Typical of movie palaces, its design elements are eclectic. Officially they are Tudor Revival, Mission Revival, and the catch-all "Other." The entry had the common flat marquee. Above that there is a four-story arched facade featuring Terra Cotta sculptures and columns and art glass windows. Like so many others it was built at the prime of the silent movie era in 1925. It became part of the National Register of Historic Places in 1986 and was designated a Chicago Landmark in 1991.

The Uptown is the largest surviving of the many neighborhood movie palaces. It can seat 4,381, making it larger than some of the downtown palaces. Its opening was celebrated with a two hundred float parade and a grand ball. 12,000 people were in line for its premiere. For fifty years or more it was a popular success in taking people away from their humdrum lives. It did survive the bad times but by the end of the 1970s attendance for films had declined so far that it was converted exclusively to a major concert venue. The list of popular performers who played at the Uptown over the years is a long one. It includes Count Basie and Duke Ellington and their orchestras. Audiences also saw Bruce Springsteen and the E Street Band, the Paul Whiteman Orchestra, The Kinks, Benny Goodman and his quintet, Bing Crosby, and Cheap Trick.

By 2016, the Uptown was closed and the subject of more than one documentary and the setting for two Hollywood films. It is the center of an effort by a citizens' group named Friends of the Uptown to preserve and restore it with the eventual dream of a re-opening.

Crosstown, the Regal Theater was built in 1928 during the Great Black Migration at 47th Street and what is now Martin Luther King, Jr. Drive in the heart of Bronzeville. It featured films, dance, live music, and comedy. The Regal was the most important venue in Chicago for the presentation of Black artists. The Uptown also had an impressive list of stars who played there, but, on review, most of them were white. The list was different at the Regal. Nearly all the stars were the most prestigious acts among Black performers and it gave a platform for new ones.

The Regal was also important because all of its employees were Black. This was important during the period of movie palaces because the Black population were generally denied employment in other houses.

The style of the Regal was one of sophistication, elegance, and understatement compared to the more flamboyant palaces. It was patterned on the Savoy Ballroom in New York City's Harlem so it was more like a night club. It had a dance floor and around 3,000 seats.

All staff members dressed in high fashion and dancers wore elaborate costumes when revues were presented. They were enhanced by a top-notch orchestra and organ playing.

While it did screen films, the Regal's specialty was presenting Black acts. More Black performers actually appeared there than at the fabled Apollo Theater in Harlem. Just a few examples of Regal performances would include Sammy Davis Jr., "Little" Stevie Wonder, Louis Armstrong, Ella Fitzgerald, Dizzy Gillespie, Miles Davis, Smoky Robinson and the Miracles, Nat "King" Cole, and the Jackson Five as an opener for other acts. B.B. King recorded one of his most popular albums *Live at the Regal* there in 1964.

Bronzeville at its best was a large part of the Harlem Renaissance, perhaps larger than Harlem itself. It didn't last, of course. The neighborhood was split by the Stevenson Expressway, adding to a decline already begun. The area became a place of drug dealing and use, gang violence, and crippling poverty.

In the past ten years, Bronzeville has enjoyed something of a gentrification but it came much too late to save the Regal. Its owner closed it and declared bankruptcy in 1968 and it was torn down in 1973. The old Regal did escape the cultural ignominy of many of the old movie palaces in becoming the site of a parking lot or retail store. Instead, it has been replaced by the Harold Washington Cultural Center, honoring Chicago's first Black mayor.

The Southtown Theatre was the last neighborhood movie palace built in Chicago. It appeared at a reported cost of $1,000,000 just as the economy was bottoming out in the Depression. It was built on 63rd St. near S. Wallace Ave. It was designed by Rapp and Rapp, the same firm which was responsible for the Uptown. Not surprisingly, like the Uptown, it was a part of the Balaban & Katz chain, but this time with an additional partner, Publix Theaters.

The Southtown is an example of many structures in history which represent the epitome of the type in their era just in time to see the era end. It seated over 3,000 in its auditorium and balcony. In the smaller of two lobbies was a feature no other movie palace downtown or in any other neighborhood could claim. It was called the Flamingo Pool which was adorned with a fountain, waterfall, live fish, and occasionally ducks. It was such a stunner that reportedly it held up the movement of people to their seats. On the mezzanine level were dioramas depicting some of the events in Chicago history. There was also a larger, multi-storied Grand Lobby and not one but two ticket booths to speed the entry of the huge crowds hoped for. There was a children's playroom, a woman's lounge, a men's lounge, and a grand staircase leading to yet another grand foyer and then to the huge auditorium and gracefully sloping balcony.

The Southtown's motif was described as Spanish-Moorish inside and out. A central feature of every movie theater was an impressive and elaborate organ. Most of these had a three-rank console with fifteen rows of pipes. The Southtown excelled all others with a four-console organ with twenty rows of pipes. The Southtown closed in 1958, somewhat earlier than other movie palaces. It was demolished in 1991 and replaced by a department store, then a flea market, perhaps a case of, "The bigger they are, the harder (or farther) they fall."

One more movie palace which deserves a description for its design is the Patio. Architectural historians call it Neo-Pompeiian with Spanish and Italian accents. If that sounds incongruous, most people who went there weren't bothered by the combination. In fact, they were enthralled by the whole effect. The theme of the auditorium was to make audience members feel as if they weren't inside at all but in a Spanish/Roman amphitheater. The walls were decorated with columns and other faux effects. The ceiling was the final element. Instead of a mammoth, elaborate ceiling fixture, the ceiling was plain and painted a simple dark blue. A special projector displayed a series of slow-moving clouds simulating an open sky. So far, the Patio has survived more than one closing by being repurposed as a specialty house for a film society, film festivals, and other special events.

The first Chicago neighborhood movie palaces opened just over a century ago. Nearly all replaced older businesses on the same site. From an early few they multiplied to several hundred providing popular entertainment at precisely the right places and in precisely the right era.

They became part and parcel of determining the culture of the times. They deftly and successfully fulfilled their mission of taking people away from a harsh or dreary life by giving them a fantastic environment and the finest in a wide variety of entertainments. Now they have entered decades when the roles have been reversed because they have outlived their original purposes. Unless they have been re-invented, they are in turn being replaced by newer business more attuned to residents' needs. Like much that's been lost in American architecture, they were too grand to last.

12

"LAUGH YOUR TROUBLES AWAY"

THRILLS AND CHILLS AT
RIVERVIEW AMUSEMENT PARK

For three generations of Chicagoans and those who lived nearby the address, Western & Belmont was synonymous with Riverview Amusement Park. The very thought of being there brought a thrill of anticipation. Actually being there brought chills of daring bravery for children and adults who rode frightening rides or walked through its fun houses.

Everything you could want was there. You could find a free, shady picnic grove, and food and drink concessions. If so inclined, you could roller skate at an indoor rink or dance at the large dance pavilion. There were games of skill and chance, shows of historical significance or of the latest technology, and, of course, rides galore, from the gentle to those with threatening reputations. And all so inexpensive and easy to reach that any family could go through the gates for a day of fun.

Riverview Amusement Park had its origin in the late 1800s as Sharpshooters (Schuetzen) Park. Its twenty-two acres of forested land was owned by Wilhelm (William) Schmidt, a wealthy German-American baker. It was a place for other German-Americans who filled the nearby neighborhoods to take target practice. During the first ten years, Sharpshooters Park was a male-only preserve and far enough out in the country for shooting to be safe.

By 1904, enough pressure had been brought on the club members that it was opened to families. There was a picnic grove, concessions for beer and wine, and a children's playground. It was located on a bend in the Chicago River which had not long before been so successfully reversed.

Because of its location and facilities, Sharpshooters Park quickly became popular with all of the many German-American societies in the city. Soon other social and political groups were paying to use the park. With its financial success and large crowds, shooting was ended. In 1904 the name was changed to Riverview Sharpshooters Park. The confines of the park were expanded to 102 acres and became a center for military bands so popular in that era. Opening Day in 1904 featured the playing of the German Imperial Marine Band and drew a crowd of over 30,000.

William's son, George Schmidt, had gone on a European tour after his college graduation. On his trip, he stopped at Copenhagen's Tivoli Gardens and New York City's Luna Park amusement parks. He thought the north side of Chicago would enjoy a park similar to the South Side's San Souci and White City. George asked his father for a small section of Sharpshooters Park for his idea. He got that permission and soon had a small park with a few concessions and three rides.

George's experiment was so popular that the area was expanded. With two partners he leased the new park to concessionaires for ten years at $7600/year. When the ten successful years were up, George and his father took over the rides and concessions. George rapidly expanded them in number and variety. The fence separating the amusement park from the picnic grove was taken down which greatly increased attendance and acreage. At that time, the park reached its maximum size of 140 acres. Families could now come to one place for a full day of fun. The changes in focus were reflected in name changes. In 1910 Sharpshooters was dropped and Exhibition was added. In 1913 the final name change was made to Riverview Amusement Park.

The Schmidts adopted their own pricing structure at Riverview. There was a nominal admission fee and the public paid an additional small fee for each ride and attraction. This gave patrons the choice

Entrance to Riverview Amusement Park. (Courtesy of the Wikimedia Commons public domain.)

of spending only a small amount for the whole day. The picnic grove was always free. Some rides were owned and operated by independent concessionaires who were responsible to keep up a high standard of safety, appearance, and honesty. They were also responsible for their own insurance and maintenance costs. A percentage of earnings would be paid to the Schmidt's.

George Schmidt was insistent on bringing in new attractions and rides. He had the park's first roller coaster built, "The Figure Eight." It used steam power to raise the coaster cars to the top of an incline. As the cars descended mildly downhill, they were controlled by a series of checks. Riders described the ride as "exhilarating" and "as if we were going like sixty." Instead the ride was short and reached a maximum speed of 24 mph.

The two merry-go-rounds at Riverview were, first, a forty-five-foot model. Then the Schmidt family commissioned the construction of an elaborate pavilion to house the Fairyland Merry-Go-Round. Inside was a fabulous carousel. It had seventy horses, both jumpers and stationary, plus ornately carved seats for two or three riders who wanted to sit close to each other. The horses were each individually carved from solid blocks of wood by German, Swiss, Austrian, and Italian carvers, then painted in elaborate designs so no two were exactly the same. Millions rode it over the years. It was so popular that it was one of only two Riverview rides to survive the destruction of the park. It was saved by a collector in Woodstock, Illinois who hoped to reconstruct it there. When that plan failed it was sold again and can now be found at Six Flags Atlanta with the name Riverview Carousel.

Riverview was no stranger to hard times. The first came during WWI when anti-German sentiment kept crowds away. In the '30s, the park faced not only The Great Depression but also the Chicago Century of Progress World's Fair on the lakefront in 1933-34. Riverview survived by cutting its fees. Two cent days and five cent nights were initiated and lasted for years. During these special days, rides were shortened and food portions were reduced. The hot dog on a roll, first introduced at Riverview, was reduced to two inches in length but still reserved for Oscar Mayer's sausages because he was a personal friend of the Schmidt family. During the Depression, George Schmidt worked for a salary of a dollar a year. Up to 700,000 passes were given out annually. During the Depression, a sizable portion of Riverview's property was sold to the Chicago Board of Education for the construction of Lane Technical High School. During WWII reduced fees were offered to those in uniform and little prejudice toward German connected businesses was apparent, helping keep attendance high.

From its first days, Riverview was a popular spot for political rallies. Republicans, Democrats, and splinter parties all met there. Theodore Roosevelt spoke there. So did "Big Bill" Haywood, founder and presidential candidate of the International Workers of the World who drew 80,000 in one of the largest recorded daily attendances.

The mayor of Chicago, William Hale Thompson, also called "Big Bill" was a special friend of the Schmidts and Riverview. One day every year he closed public schools and paid for the admission of students. He passed out thousands of copies of the Constitution. He also commissioned the building of a luxury yacht on the Chicago River at Riverview.

During Prohibition, city inspectors were told to ignore liquor sales in the park and picnic grove. There was also a free admission day once a year for newsboys. Large clubs and businesses like Ford and Crane often bought out the park to give their employees a day of free fun.

Riverview was a pioneer of roller coaster standards for all contemporary amusement parks and those in the future. Safety in construction and testing were rigorous. Each morning the cars were loaded with sandbags and the ride operator rode it alone around the track. Pneumatic braking and other designs were incorporated first at Riverview. At one time or another, there were eight roller coasters at the park. The tamest was the appropriately named Velvet Coaster, which hit a top speed of seven mph. The park also offered coasters named the Blue Streak, the Silver Flash, the Comet, the Greyhound, the Fireball, and best of all, the Bobs.

The author rode the Bobs on several occasions. Because the cars had no canopy like the other roller coasters in the park, it was misleading. It seemed safe until you rode the clanking, jerking cars to the top of the first downhill. After that, the cars roared and twisted at what seemed like a maniacal velocity. In reality the highest speed achieved at the bottom of a slope was 43 mph. The illusion of speed was made by placing the support railings within a few feet of the track, an innovation introduced at Riverview.

The cars had only a lap bar for stability for passengers so it was definitely not a so-called "hands up" ride as is found in many parks today. In fact, there were sadly two fatalities on the Bobs both caused by riders trying to stand up and being hurled from a car. There were two positions which were greatly favored by riders of the Bobs. One was the front seat as you got to be the first to see and feel everything. The second favorite was at the opposite end where the last seats gave the roughest and bumpiest ride. Since the first ride cost only a nickel or dime and a second ride as little as two cents, a person might have to wait longer to get a seat that others also liked. The Bobs usually had 700,000 first riders and 300,000 second rides annually. The author could make a footnote that riding the Bobs made him unafraid to ride any other roller coaster at any other park until well into his sixties.

There were many other rides and attractions at Riverview. Some lasted for decades, some for only a few years. A short list would include a Tilt-A-Whirl, the Pair-O-Chutes, and three miniature railroads (first steam, later diesel). The Sky Ride was a cable car which soared over the park. Witching Waters gave the sensation of driving though on an undulating belt. Of course there was also a bumper car ride and a water-borne version as well. The Aquarousel gave a gentle spin in a swan boat. Under the Sea created the illusion of an underwater adventure. There was also a pair of giant swings. One had multiple single seats. The other was a single car that swung gradually through a larger and larger arc. Today this ride is found at the best traveling carnivals and might be called The Phoenix. There were two tours through simulated scenery, The Thousand Islands and Scenic Railway. It was fitting for Chicago that a 150-foot Ferris wheel was there. The Caterpillar was especially popular with couples since it was a mild ride and soon after it began, it was covered by a canopy darkening the inside.

Two rides were purchased from the 1933 Century of Progress World's Fair. One was the Rotor. This ride was really scary because as it rotated faster and faster centrifugal force pinned riders to the wall and the floor dropped away. It was the other ride purchased when the park closed. It was installed at another amusement park but was removed because it really did cause injuries. The Flying Turns was a simulated bobsled run. The forces involved were so great in the curves that they had to be buttressed. When you rode it, you thought the cars would fly over the edge of each curve and crash. Naturally, it never happened.

One facet of all the scary rides at Riverview was typified by the Shoot-the-Chutes. This was a ride in which a gondola boat was hoisted to the top of a long slide and dropped to a lagoon below. Inside the tunnel to the hoist one could see what looked like rickety and rotting support timbers. The ride on the hoist seemed jerky and slipped. In addition, water was constantly dripping inside. Like all the roller coasters, the Chutes and the other scary rides were actually so solidly built and well-maintained that a wrecking ball had to be brought in to bring them down when the park was closed.

It wouldn't have been Riverview without concessions. There was always a sideshow featuring sword swallowers, fire-eaters, magicians, and double-jointed contortionists. There was always a place for "freaks." Nowadays, in a less tolerant time, this is seen as cruel; but back then, it did have the saving advantage of providing employment for those with physical abnormalities like the Fat Lady, the Strong Man, the Giant, and the Tattooed Lady.

True to its origins as Sharpshooters Park, Riverview had a shooting gallery where patrons could fire real .22 rifles at targets. Another shooting gallery featured machine guns which shot BBs in a rapid stream.

Riverview had two funhouses over the years. The Bug House, sacred to the author's father's memory, burned to the ground in the 1930s. It was replaced by a huge building named Aladdin's Castle. The outside featured a giant genie with a turban and rolling eyes. Inside were distorting mirrors, a confusing maze of screen doors, a rolling barrel to stumble through, and a collapsing seat and slide down to the floor below. The traditional air jets in the floors weren't forgotten. A fun house like Aladdin's Castle brings up another benefit of Riverview—employment. Hundreds worked there at any one season (The park was closed in winter for maintenance and construction). There were dozens working in just the fun house. Even Walt Disney worked at Riverview when he was a boy in Chicago.

It may be somewhat surprising to know that among all the thrilling rides and attractions the Schmidts empathized education as well. History was shown in the cyclorama Battle of the *Monitor* and *Merrimac*. Riverview was one of the first venues for motion pictures and its "instant" photography of visitors having a good time was popular. Exhibitions used the most up-to-date technology. As stated, famous speakers came there. Rides like the Scenic Railway gave geographic views of areas that average citizens would never visit. As shameful as we might view it in the twenty-first century, there was an encampment of Native Americans. A similar exhibit was the Igurrotes village of natives from the Philippines. This exhibit had already appeared earlier at the 1909 Alaska/Yukon/Pacific World's Fair in Seattle where at least part of the controversial attraction was that possibility of gawking at half-naked villagers. Hopefully some learned the culture of unfamiliar groups. There was a Wild West Show starring the real-life cowboy and film star Tom Mix who was paid $1.50/hour when he wasn't making a film at the Chicago Essany Studios.

If Riverview was able to overcome some adversities such as two world wars, a ten-year depression, lakefront fairs, and labor strife, there were also factors beyond its ability to respond. With the 1950s came trends which dramatically affected the park. As ethnic Whites in Chicago moved to the suburbs, the neighborhoods around the park changed. A trip to Riverview for a family from a far suburb was not nearly so cheap, quick, or comfortable as a trolley ride. Television was not only a threat to the film industry; people who might have come to Riverview for an evening of inexpensive fun could now have as much fun comfortably at home.

Riverview was always a leader in building new rides and attractions. By the '50s, these had become much more expensive. The 1959 Fireball roller coaster cost the Schmidts almost a half-million dollars and the Skyway ride another quarter million. Maintenance costs were also rising fast. Employees at the park were all union workers and were making $11.00/hr, a large wage for unskilled labor fifty years ago. Costs of insurance, taxes, even food and liquor, also increased. Raising prices to garner more profit only caused a drop in attendance.

In addition, the make-up of crowds in the park was changing. The park had never been welcoming to minorities. At one time there was a minstrel show there and a dunking tank where people of color were the targets. Roving groups of youths came to the park looking for trouble. Even in the days before drugs, gangs, and guns, there was often violence and the park police force had to be increased. The park was no longer thought to be a safe place for families, especially at night. And you could add the coming of theme parks in the late 1950s as well. These new places of entertainment made Riverview look shabby and dated.

Despite all the problems, few expected the end to be so abrupt. In 1967 the Board of Directors agreed to sell the park to the Arvey Corporation. George Schmidt objected strenuously, but he was a minority stockholder by then, though still executive director of park operations. When the sale was announced on radio, television, and in the papers, it created shock and storms of protest. Editorials, broadcasts, pleading, and even threatening letters were of no avail; the sale was final. The former site of Riverview now contains the Riverview Plaza Shopping Mall, DeVry University, a police precinct, and Richard Clark Park. The picnic grove is still there, and at one end of the park, the foundations of rides and buildings can be seen.

For more than fifty years, as was advertised on radio, in print, on television, billboards, in theaters, and on streetcars, Riverview Amusement Park was the place to "Laugh Your Troubles Away." It was a pioneer of similar parks in the future. You can find echoes of Riverview at the Six Flags Parks, Hershey Park, Cedar Point, and others. It's not going too far to think that it might have been an inspiration for Walt Disney when he dreamed up Disneyland and Disney World. Riverview Amusement Park lives on only in its influence on its successors and in the memories of those who enjoyed it.

13

A CAPTAIN'S NATION

STREETERVILLE

Chicago has surely had its share of oddball characters, maybe more than its share. Corrupt politicians like "Hinky Dink" Kenna and "Bathhouse John" Coughlin, America's first serial killer H.H. Holmes, eccentric builders such as Washington Porter, Jr, unscrupulous business tycoons like Samuel Insull, a cranky goat-owning saloon-keeper named Sianis who put a seventy-year curse on the Cubs, and gangsters galore.

Most Chicagoans, but almost no others, have at least heard of one, if for no other reason than that the most desirable and exclusive neighborhood in the city bears his name. An outrageous, opportunistic, defiant, and troublesome character who was a thorn in the side of the city police, politicians, and land developers for thirty years. His name was George Streeter and his strange story and ironic claims make for another interesting Chicago tale.

We have to go back to the days before Chicago was not much more than a fur trading post. A combination of geology, or more accurately, Lake Michigan currents caused the mouth of the Chicago River to silt over with sand bars as quickly as a channel could be cleared. One of the largest was 450 yards off the true lake shore. It became a haven for squatters and illegal practices including the sale of alcohol on Sundays. In 1857 all of the neer-do-wells were evicted by police as ordered by the mayor.

Depending on which version of the tales you prefer, George Streeter and his common-law wife, Maria, had acquired a rickety old schooner named *Reutan* by 1886. Their plan was to sail her to Latin America to run guns and other cargo, but on a shake-down cruise, *Reutan* wound up stranded on that sand bar. Streeter always claimed he was blown off course by a storm but weather records show no indication of bad winds that night. Some would later say that the Streeters had planned the whole thing as the beginning of an audacious scheme to gain attention and make money through extortion. If so, he had the training for it. Though he actually did serve in the Civil War, he was never a captain. Otherwise he had been a showman, circus promoter, and lumberman. He evidently took the nickname "Cap" for himself as a riverboat pilot on the Mississippi.

Cap and Maria liked the off-shore location of the *Reutan* so much they decided it would make a good, if temporary, home and decided to stay put. They dismissed the crew and threw themselves on the mercy of the sandbar's owner N. Kellogg Fairbank who gave the humble and persuasive Streeter permission to stay on the *Reutan* until it could be repaired and re-floated. This kindly deed began to bring trouble—lots of trouble.

Soon Cap and Maria had moved off the *Reutan* and built a shack from its pieces. He promptly and proudly announced that since he wasn't actually on shore, the sandbar was his and he had sovereignty over it and that only the federal government had jurisdiction. He based his claims on a fraudulent land survey and forged documents which he was convinced were signed by Grover Cleveland. He proclaimed he was establishing the "Deestrict (sic) of Lake Michigan."

Before you knew it, Streeter had set himself up as a real estate investor in a fancy office in the exclusive Tremont Hotel and was soon doing, if you'll excuse the expression, a "land-office business," selling lots at bargain prices in his district. His sales prices were purposely undervalued and speculators knew it. His many clients, both greedy and gullible, were willing to take a chance.

"Cap" Streeter and his wife, possibly Maria.

If this isn't already sounding like the first act of a comic opera, the city and its developers awoke to the fact that the land would skyrocket in value after the first Michigan Ave. bridge was finished. The city sent five constables to evict Cap and Maria but were faced with a rifle. Perhaps it was a bluff but the constables retreated in disarray. Round one went to Cap.

In August of 1886, five more and most likely different constables showed up unannounced and laid hands on Cap, boasting "Now we got 'cha!" Not the end, you might have guessed, and you'd be right, for the good Mrs. Streeter emerged from the shack with a pot of scalding water that she poured on the constables. Cap was able to get his rifle and the boys-in-blue ran for it. Round two to the Streeters.

Between rounds, Cap appointed Wm. Niles as his "military governor." Niles used his own rifle to take pot shots at a police captain's buggy. This was such a humiliating and egregious affront to their dignity that the police and their hired thugs came back five hundred strong the very next day. They were met by Streeter's army of hobos and proprietors of gambling halls, drinking establishments, and houses of ill repute throwing rocks and bottles (all of which were empty). The force retreated with Cap as a prisoner. Charged with a crime, "Cap" walked because no one could find an ordinance which made shooting at a policeman a crime. The judge also found that Cap's army had acted in self-defense. This would become a common plea for his "army" after its periodic arrests. Round three to Cap.

Finally, Mayor "Big Bill" Thompson had had enough. If Streeter and his gang of toughs couldn't be locked up for trespassing, they could be arrested for illicit liquor sales, gambling, and prostitution. He ordered a raid in which hundreds of beer bottles were seized (full this time) and Cap's shack burned to the ground. Cap was ornery on a good day, but this time his fury knew no bounds. He was already the darling of the press because his latest escapades and brushes with the law made good copy. With full press coverage, he cried "This here is an outrage! It's worse than the Kaiser ever did! I'll have the law on them!" A bit of irony there, to be sure, and it wasn't missed by his many fans who had adopted him as the classic underdog, the beleaguered loner, fighting the good fight. A David vs. Goliath if you want to carry it far enough. (Cap gets a Pyrrhic win.)

In 1893, the same gullible Fairbank who had helped Streeter in his perceived predicament filed suit and Cap was ordered evicted from his beloved "Deestrict" but not without another fight. He vowed "to raise an army" and blockade any attempt to make him leave. His motley troops deserted him, moving to vice zones elsewhere. After all they had been paying Cap for his allowing their illegal businesses and they didn't want a bigger fight. His faction of supporters at home turned out to be an armchair army and offered nothing but sympathy. Once off his sandbar, Cap was jailed for manslaughter in 1890 when he killed a night watchman whom he claimed was a "trespasser," but he was out after two years. He never again set foot on his sandbar home, which by 1893 was no longer disconnected from the shoreline, the water having been filled it by rubble from Chicago's rapid expansion much of which Cap himself paid to have dumped to expand his territory knowing that it would now be much more valuable. (Cap was now on the ropes.)

That's the legendary version of Cap's story. The other side, the one which emerges in the many court proceedings, is more calculating.

Testimony showed that the District was a swindle from the first. There was never a plan to run guns with the *Reutan*: no storm, no land survey, or papers from the president. His squatting and defiant fight was all part of an extortion plan to get powerful landowners to buy him out. A confederate stated that Cap told him, "They'll have to buy me out. We'll make a million."

Cap wasn't done fighting and the suits and counter-suits continued until his death from pneumonia in 1921 at the age of eighty-four. Even then his heirs continued the legal quagmire until the courts finally awarded the titles to the land to Fairbank and Chicago Title and Trust in 1940.

Streeter may have been one of the earliest to see the potential of the sandbar, especially after it was connected to land, thus his elaborate con job, but he was far from the last. Land-owners and developers with names which still recall the epitome of Chicago wealth and power, Potter Palmer, the Fairbank and Farwell families, the estate of Chicago's first mayor Wm. Ogden, and Chicago Title and Trust are just a few. It was less than a decade after the Columbian Exhibition so there was still great incentive to fulfill Burnham's plan for Chicago. That meant extending and improving Michigan Ave with a new bridge to Lincoln Park. By then the area that was already being called Streeterville was limited to warehouses and small factories. There were only a few mansions and luxury row houses which that been built to take advantage of the lakefront panorama.

Though the legal battles officially ended in 1940, development was put on hold soon after starting due to WWII with its material shortages and dim views of private development. During the post-war boom, there was no more recognizable nor influential name in Chicago real-estate development than Arthur Rubloff. He and his partners were responsible for creating not only the concept but the reality of Michigan Avenue's Magnificent Mile including the very symbol of Chicago's survival and resurgence after the Great 1871 Fire, the historic Water Tower. Now, instead of landfill, it is one of the city's "concrete canyons" where the sun shines directly only a few hours a day.

Rubloff and others rushed to develop Streeterville with its ideal location near Michigan Ave, the coming Outer Drive and unparalleled lakefront vistas. Today there is no more desirable neighborhood in Chicago than Streeterville. Inside its boundaries can be found some of the city's tallest towers, The John Hancock Center at 1,127'; 900 N. Michigan, 871'; Water Tower Place, 859'; River East, 644'; Lake Point Tower, 645'; and ten more at 500' or taller.

Cap Streeter's "Deestrict" is no longer but Streeterville now has another, more honorable recognition as an official Historic District. What can be found there? You could start with Tribune Tower, the Drake Hotel, 4th Presbyterian Church, Navy Pier, and the site of the home of John Baptiste DuSable, Chicago's founder. One landmark is the 1930s constructed tower now renamed the Palmolive Building, but for years better known as the headquarters of Playboy Enterprises. Atop the Palmolive Building is the Lindbergh Beacon, once a guide for aircraft seen for many miles. Now it has been darkened because its blinding rays were disturbing the sleep of tenants in taller buildings nearby.

Not just high-rises, apartments, and condominiums occupy Streeterville though. Northwestern University has its Pritzker School of Law and Kellogg School of Business. The University of Chicago has its own Booth School of Business. Close-by are Northwestern Hospital, The Ann and Robert Lurie Children's Hospital, the Rehabilitation Institute of Chicago, Prentice Women's Hospital, and Fineberg School of Medicine.

The rewards of living in Streeterville these days aren't limited to beyond-first-class residences. An equally upscale ambiance of living has come with it. If you can afford to live there you will be able to shop at the choicest shops and stores, gain membership in the most exclusive clubs, and dine in the trendiest of restaurants. Nightlife is vibrant with hardly a limit on variety. Taverns, bars, and brew pubs abound. The famed Second City Club has nearby locations, as do other locales for nightlife entertainment.

As desirable as all this sounds, it misses the true raison de vivre for Streeterville's popularity, its location on the prettiest part of the lakefront. Fine beaches can be found from North Avenue all the way up to Lincoln

Park. Through one of the underpasses beneath Lake Shore Drive, you will be only a short walk or bike ride to the fabulous Lake Front Trail and all it leads to.

Though a man of vision in his way, Ol' Cap Streeter would find it incomprehensible to be sure. However, he could take some solace in seeing the same potential he saw in the location magnified in geometric proportions. He would certainly acknowledge what had happened to his humble District of Lake Michigan and consider that he short-changed himself and was quite a "piker" when he claimed a century ago, "We'll make a million!"

14

THE RIVER NOW RUNS
TO THE SEA

Y ou sometimes read that at its source an important river "rises" to begin
its flow through history. The Cumberland, the Susquehanna, or even
the Illinois are a few. The same will never be said about the Chicago River.
It seems strange to even hear the words "the Mighty Chicago River," yet
in American history, it is as significant as the others.

It seems a bit disappointing to learn the Chicago more or less trickles
to begin its gathering of waters. It's not very impressive; there are no
rapids or falls to overcome. Not much of it in its short 150-mile course
is even navigable. Yet no one seriously questions it as one of the Great
Rivers of America because without it, the powerful city which shares its
name would not exist.

Every river has one or more sources. The Chicago River's sources
form northwest of the city in Lake and McHenry counties. There a West
Fork joins a North Fork to form the North Branch. It then meanders
through a series of sloughs, wetlands, and small ponds including the
Skokie Lagoons. Much of the shoreline in the upper part of the river has
been improved by being restored to resemble what it originally was—a
gentle stream suitable for canoes and kayaks. Along the shore, paths have
been built for walking, biking, and bird watching. Small parks attract

families for picnics. However, fishermen are warned not to eat their catch so everything is not perfect. The closer to the city the river comes the more engineered it is. Canals empty into and out of it. The course has been channelized and re-shaped to increase the volume of its flow.

If the Chicago River has a short course, it has a long, rich human history. Native Americans came and went to the area where the river once flowed into Lake Michigan. It became a seasonal home to migrant groups like the Pottawatomie. Here was where goods from the Eastern Woodlands culture were exchanged for those from other cultures. A well-established trade route known as the Grand Portage passed through the area. Important social interactions between tribal groups, councils for war and peace, and religious rites were also held in this place.

The river itself was an invaluable resource to the Native Americans who used it for drinking, bathing, cooking, cleaning, and travel. Its waters were an important source of food and its wetlands were a perfect growing medium for the wild onions or garlic which gave the area not only its name but its particular aroma. The Native Americans called it shikaakwa, the French Checagou. Either way, it meant "stinking onion." They prized the herb as it was one of the few plants available to them for seasoning. Even the weather close to the big lake was an attraction as it was warmer in the winter and cooler in the summer.

The first white men to enter the area were French fur trappers and traders who exchanged highly prized European trade goods for pelts which brought a premium price among the elite of several European nations. These first Europeans had a history of good relationships with the Native American groups because they took the time to learn their languages and appreciate their cultures. They also knew that their livelihood depended on maintaining this mutual respect.

This cooperative life abruptly ended with the first arrival of American pioneers in the first decades of the nineteenth century with their long traditions of private land ownership and conflict with Native Americans. Relations with the Native Americans soon became adversarial instead of cooperative. Ft. Dearborn was the first attempt at a permanent White settlement at the mouth of the river. It was a hastily and poorly thought-out stockade providing settlers refuge during the periodic threats of Indian savagery. The military contingent at Ft. Dearborn was poorly led, undisciplined, inexperienced, and resentful at their remote posting.

The worst threat to the fort and its huddled inhabitants came during the War of 1812 when Indian groups allied with the British fought to reverse American encroachment on their lands. Under a flag of truce, the fort's soldiers and civilians were escorted away by five hundred Pottawatomie. Almost as soon as they left the fort, they were attacked by other Pottawatomie who were not included in the councils of peace. Though a few Whites were saved by friendly Indians, more than a hundred men, women, and children were killed in the massacre. It took years for the white settlers to return and when they did, they found themselves again threatened by an Indian uprising in the Black Hawk War. The result was quite different as an American militia was able to defeat the Indians and force a treaty upon them which gave virtually all the Indian land over to White settlement.

The location of the weak little city of Chicago as a transportation center, as it was used by the Native Americans, became the engine of growth for the early city founded in 1833. It was the greatest benefactor of the completion of the Erie Canal eight years earlier. Now the Great Lakes with their many fine protected harbors connected them to not only the Eastern seaboard but, by extension, with all the European trade that plied the Atlantic. The completion of the Illinois & Michigan Canal in 1848 opened Chicago to a safe and seamless route through the Des Plaines Divide to the Illinois River, the Mississippi, and the ports of the Gulf of Mexico.

Sailing ships left the prospering new city loaded with lumber from the forests of Wisconsin or inexpensive corn and wheat from the growing number of Midwestern farms. Some specialized in carrying Chicago-packed meats from western ranches preserved by ice cut from local rivers and lakes and stored in gigantic ice houses which dotted the city. The river became vital as a route to supply inland industry with raw materials and carry out finished products. Just as it eventually became the crossroads of rail travel later in the nineteenth century and air travel in the next two centuries, it was first a crossroads of shipping. By mid-century, the Chicago exports included increasing amounts of Chicago farm implements and other manufactured goods. At first, ships returned with cargoes of Eastern goods for sale but it wasn't long before they began returning filled with immigrants and penniless easterners seeking employment and a better life.

Immigrants came to Chicago for the same reasons they had always come to America, for religious freedom, economic opportunity, and to escape political oppression in their various homelands. Chicago's location at the merge of what was left of the great eastern forests and the vast Midwestern prairie brought thousands of failed farmers from the east where the combination of thin rocky soil, harsh weather, and competition from cheaper Midwestern products made agriculture desperately hard. They dreamed of starting anew in the rich soil and moderate environment of the prairies.

The greatest source of Chicago immigration for more than a century was from European nations. Refugees came in tidal waves of Irish, German, Italian, Czech, Polish, and other Eastern European countries. A curious fact is that at one time the second leading city of Polish-speaking citizens was Chicago.

Depending on the time when they arrived and how quickly they were assimilated, the second and third generations of original immigrants found a successful place in Chicago. The Irish dominated politics with mayors named Kelly, Kenelly, and two named Daley. The Germans and other Northern Europeans formed the first working and business classes dominating the economic opportunities with shops and factories. By the time Poles, Italians, and Czechs arrived with their poor education and command of English, the only employment readily available was a factory laborer or increasingly in stockyards and meat packing houses. People of common origin gathered in neighborhoods for mutual support and tradition. That's why there is a Little Italy, a little Warsaw, and a Czech Village in Chicago. The thought of a Little Ireland or German Village in Chicago is hard to imagine.

With the arrival of so many mostly poverty-stricken residents, the condition of the Chicago River declined from serious to critical. In its unregulated growth, little time was spent in civic planning. The unpaved streets and ultimately the river became the city's de facto sewer system. City fathers recognized the problems and in mid-nineteenth century embarked on an unprecedented civil engineering project to prevent the frequent flooding of city streets and the raw sewage running in them. It was a stunning concept for the time or any time. Instead of trying to lay new infrastructure in the swampy soil on which the city had been built, the entire city was raised from seven to seventeen feet.

Every building was raised and a new foundation built underneath it. The sewers and water mains were laid out on the old street surface and buried by fill. Even the largest buildings of four or five stories were incrementally raised while still being used. (The chief engineer was a young man with a bright future named George Pullman.) In the older neighborhoods, you can still see houses with stairways to the second story remaining from the work.

While the immense project did solve many problems, it did little good for the river except concentrate where the effluents entered. Reeking odors persisted. It must have been like living in the outhouse. Everyone had to put up with the stench, even those away from the river. What residents couldn't tolerate were the frequent epidemics that swept the city. No longer was the disease the mosquito-borne malaria because the surrounding swamps had been drained. The new epidemics were even more deadly: typhoid fever, cholera, and dysentery. They were truly non-discriminatory for while they were more virulent in the city slums, they also struck down the wealthy in their neighborhoods.

At the time, medical science largely ignored or was ignorant of the germ theory of illness. While contagion was obvious, polluted water was not suspect. The fear of contagion even spread to the dead. All but one of the bodies from the city cemetery was disinterred and re-buried in rural cemeteries like Rose Hill and Graceland.

By the 1890s, river water was no longer the source of the city's drinking water. Instead, water came from intakes on the shore of Lake

Michigan where it was thought certain to be purer. One measure is that it didn't smell as bad and it looked clean. In fact, it was where families came to escape the city's dirt, heat, and clamor.

Medical science had for years been able to microscopically examine a drop of water and see what lived therein. Some of those organisms were proven to be bacteria which caused the epidemics that plagued Chicago. Someone with authority (Hopefully with the sanitation department.) ordered testing of the lake water and found it polluted too. It was one of those things that someone should have considered earlier but didn't. The volumes of river water were mixing with the lake water and contaminating it as well.

Solutions were sought. The city couldn't be moved and there was nothing that could be done to fix the river, but there was all of that pure, safe water farther off-shore. In one of those "Eureka" hydrological moments engineers asked each other if the waters of the river could be made to flow away from the lake instead of into it. Then all the contaminants would be flushed downstream toward the Illinois River and become someone else's problem. If you planned big and bold enough you could create huge new systems of locks and channels to increase freight flow from Chicago to the Illinois and Mississippi Rivers without off-loading from one boat to another.

Once they stumbled on the concept, they realized the Illinois-Michigan Canal had proven it more than a half-century before. Through its combination of locks, dams, channels, and canals it had crossed the Des Plaines Divide. At the same time engineers knew that the I-M Canal was much too narrow and shallow to carry the flow from the river that was necessary

Work began in 1892. Locks were installed at the mouth of the Chicago River and the Calumet River, which would also be reversed. To make the idea work well enough, amounts of water would have to be drawn off the lake and routed south and west. With the completion of the Cal-Sag Channel and the Chicago Sanitary and Ship Canal in 1909, not only could the necessary flow be maintained but barge tows could be moved from the Chicago area ports directly to the Mississippi. The channels had to be very large. For the basis of comparison, the I-M Canal was 6 feet deep and 60 feet wide. The Chicago Sanitary and Ship Canal is 180 feet wide and 9 feet deep without the problems of silt infiltration that plagued the old canal.

The reversing of the Chicago River has been deservedly deemed one of the marvels of the engineering world, but it only solved part of the problem. Next was to determine how much water was to be taken from the lake. Too little and the river would not flow as strongly as it could. The level of the river had to be kept at a relative level of two to five feet below the lake level. If too much lake water or too much run-off from torrential rains caused the river level to rise above the lake level the river would again flow into the lake, in effect reversing the reversal. And, how much water could Chicago draw from the lake before it reduced the lake level and other cities who depended on a predictable, constant lake level took Chicago to federal court?

Flushing the river waste downstream in its artificial direction did rid the city of its pollution problem, but it didn't do enough to secure safe drinking water for the growing metropolitan area. Occasional surges of storm sewer water had to be sent into the lake to keep the river level correct. That meant lake shore water was still not safe. The solution was the construction of a series of water intakes from two to four miles out in the lake where the deep bottom water was sent through subterranean tunnels to the city. When the stone intake structures were being built from 1892-1935, they were surrounded by temporary coffer dams topped by wooden structures that from a distance reminded the many former rural residents of Chicago of nothing more than the corn cribs that every farm in the Midwest had for drying corn. The nickname stuck. Some of those "cribs" are still visible far out in the lake. Even many native Chicagoans don't know what they are, but now you know and can fill them in. Some of the cribs have been idled or removed as unnecessary hazards to navigation, but a few are still active. The water they pump to the city now goes to the John Jardine Water Filtration Plant near Navy Pier. It has the immense capacity to not only supply the entire metropolitan area of Cook County but those of more than twenty suburbs where forward-thinking residents approved bond issues to pay for the scores of miles of infrastructure that would bring lake water to them.

The "new" Chicago River flowing from the lake is now called the "Main Stem." This is the section of the river which is the best known as it flows south and west past some of the most iconic structures in the world including Tribune Tower, Trump Tower, Willis Tower, the Old Water Tower, the Magnificent Mile, Union Station, and Marina City, plus dozens of other structures designed by world-renown architects. Improving the river was a pet project of the first Mayor Daley, who fostered many projects to clean and beautify the riverscape. While it is far better, no one will probably ever call it clean. The downtown section has been lined with a well-planned river walk which is popular with office workers for sunny lunches and where tourists can stroll. There are pubs and small restaurants among memorial plaques to Ft. Dearborn and the SS *Eastland* disaster. Along the way, there are stairs to street level where an even greater variety of pleasures awaits. Along the walk, you can descend to water level to find excursion boats for historical and architectural cruises and water taxis from Union Station to Navy Pier. There's a safe connection to the Lake Front Trail and Museum Campus. This section of the river is known for being dyed Kelly green each year in conjunction with the largest St. Patrick's Day Parade in the world. In the fall of 2016. it was dyed blue to celebrate the Cubs' World Series Championship.

In the 1990s, the frequent problem of storm surges causing polluted water entering the lake was finally solved by the fabulously expensive and years late Deep Tunnel Project. A series of tunnels have been blasted and bored hundreds of feet below street level. From there the stormwater is sent to treatment plants and then to some of the empty stone quarries in the area. While some sections of the project have been completed, final construction will not be completed for decades.

The Chicago was an industrial river through much of its history, one of the many reasons for its pollution. It was also the reason for the city being well-known for its many bridges. In the days of sailboats, they came directly up the river with their tall masts. Surface level bridges were too low for them to pass but were necessary for street traffic. The solution was to install a movable bridge structure at each crossing. The earliest bridges were center pivot bridges. They proved to be too slow and unreliable, so they were replaced by the city's famous draw bridges. Chicago has more bridges (thirty-two) than any other city in the world except Amsterdam and by far the most draw bridges.

Most boats on the river, pleasure craft, water taxis, tour boats, and the occasional barge tow, can all easily pass under a closed bridge, but that doesn't mean the jackknife and bascule bridges don't need to open. There are dozens of true sailboats and motor-sailers that use the river to move out of winter storage in the spring and return in the fall. To keep the streets from being blocked every time a tall ship passes the park district and the city have devised a calendar for bridge openings. One weekend in each season is given over to allow the taller ships to be moved up or down river to and from their harbor moorings. That weekend has

Chicago River with most draw bridges open.

become an attraction in itself as hundreds of viewers come to the river to see so many of the bridges open at the same time. It is a memorable sight to see these beautiful expensive sailing yachts moving line astern on the river.

Tall or short, canoe or worth millions, every boat must pass through the lock to enter Lake Michigan. Here they might have to wait until the lock empties for those craft coming back to the river. When the gates swing open, all the boats crowd inside and hopefully all follow sailing etiquette. Once outside the locks, a big enough boat can, as many do, go through the Great Lakes, even to the Atlantic and beyond through the St. Lawrence Seaway. By staying on the river and using the Sanitary and Ship Canal or the Cal-Sag Canal it's only a matter of time before you can reach the Mississippi and downriver to the Gulf of Mexico, then the rest of the world.

The Chicago River will never be noted as a national treasure. It never has been nor ever will be beautiful. It does have accolades of which it can be proud. It has been a useful river for human needs for thousands of years and perhaps for many of the wrong reasons, but its value to Chicago and the nation is impossible to calculate.

15

CHICAGO'S RAILROADS SINK TO NEW DEPTHS

THE CHICAGO RR CO. CTA SUBWAY AND THE GREAT CHICAGO FLOOD

It is safe to say that among the tens of thousands of passengers who rode subways through Chicago's Loop on the first weekend of April in 1992, only a small fraction were aware of what lay twenty feet below them. It hadn't even reached the status of an urban legend. But by Monday the 4th, everybody knew.

A crew driving pilings for what is known as a "dolphin" to protect barges from bumping into the Kinzie Street bridge had, through a combination of carelessness and ignorance, weakened a wall of a largely forgotten tunnel system forty feet below the river bottom. The railroad tunnel was used for more than fifty years to service some of the most important buildings in the Loop business district including the Merchandise Mart, the world's largest office building, Marshall Field & Co's flagship store, the Federal Reserve Bank, City Hall, and the Chicago Hilton and Towers.

A cable television camera crew first discovered a slight leak in the tunnel wall and reported it. The leak caught the city off-guard. It was thought at first that the pumps which had been moving water out of the tunnel would deal with the extra leak. Within a day the pressure from the river created a "car-sized" rupture in the wall and millions of gallons of polluted river water began to spread through the building's basements ruining valuable merchandise and destroying public records.

The city had no plan to deal with this quiet catastrophe so it was slow in responding. To make matters worse, ignorance of the tunnel system allowed the flooding to spread much farther than hoped or expected. There was an evasive nature in the answers to the questions asked by the press and most information was given on the promise of anonymity. There was a lot of finger-pointing and delay over who was responsible for the flood. Several busy streets had to be closed off at a great loss to commercial businesses. Public and commercial pressure eventually caused the immediate squabbling to end and a combination of governments came together to have the leak plugged, but only at great cost. Immediately different squabbling began which lasted for years. It involved complicated legal fights over what or who was responsible for the flood and if the damage was covered by insurance. (It was.)

People across the country were fascinated by what they began to learn about the tunnel system and it does make an interesting story. They learned some important facts. The subterranean system of supply was much older than the much-beloved subway system. Like the subway, it ran on tracks and was powered by electricity. Like the subway, it went under the Chicago River in more than one spot. They found some differences as well. The tunnel railroad never carried a paying passenger and it was a true tunnel. Because it was there first, it limited the depth to which a passenger subway could be built to twenty-and-a-half feet.

That made it necessary to build the subway from the surface down. You could use a mutually exclusive term by naming it a "surface subway." Here's how that came about. There had been discussion for years about how to deal with the ever-increasing volume of traffic on the downtown streets. The streetcar and interurban lines could only do so much and took up a significant amount of street space themselves. As a result, they were the cause of some of the congestion. Something needed to be done to get thousands of cars off the streets and people back and forth to the neighborhoods with greater speed and safety. Two alternatives were

Original 1899 AT&T access tunnel showing marks from knife carvings through the surrounding clay.

tossed around. First was an expansion of the elevated or "El" tracks, the second a subway.

There were some serious problems with the El expansion. First it would affect traffic for years during construction. Second and more importantly the support structure would always be there. There was a strong push back from merchants who knew from experience that the inevitable web of support beams darkened the streets, hurt business, and caused conversations to pause as trains rumbled past. Given that some of these merchants were the most affluent and politically connected civic leaders, the El was a non-starter.

An unusual geological feature of Chicago's soil is that bedrock is much more than forty feet below the surface. The subsoil is all a thick blue clay that is impervious to moisture. That meant it would be easy and quick to excavate a huge trench for a subway. However, no rock to tunnel through meant inadequate support for the walls of a subway. Engineers decided to create an artificial tunnel using a method called "trench and fill." The concept was pretty simple. Traffic was closed on a street and the paving removed. Excavators could easily remove the clay for a huge trench. Spoil would be used to expand the lakefront. To give the subway safe support, sections of prefabricated caissons were built and laid horizontally in the trench then connected to each other. The trench could then be back-filled, the paving restored, and the street opened to traffic. The tracks and third rail power source could be installed afterward.

It was a good system but by the 1930s, Chicago could not build it alone. The city was far in debt due to the Great Depression. Chicago was (and is) a Democratic stronghold and with the New Deal in firm control of the federal government, it wasn't long before construction of the subway became a showpiece for the New Deal "make-work" programs, Works Progress Administration and Public Works Administration, which also built airports, dams, roads, paved streets and built post offices and courthouses across the country to keep the money flowing. With the influx of federal help, the subway system made rapid progress and was completed by 1943.

Meanwhile, nineteen-and-one half feet below, the new subway work the Chicago Railroad Co. was still in service and, in fact, still being expanded. It too had originally been planned to alleviate crowding on surface streets but this time not to limit traffic. In 1899, Illinois Telephone and Telegraph wanted to bring its services into the downtown business district, but they had a problem. The streets were already full of utility poles for the distribution of electricity. The city denied the application. AT&T engineers inspected the underground area and found the same blue clay that lay close to the surface. They saw that it would be easy to carve a small tunnel just to accommodate their cables. Only unskilled workers with draw knives were needed to carve the walls and ceiling. The tunnel only needed to be large enough to allow access for a worker and the cable equipment which would be directed through manhole covers on the surface. Or, at least, that's how the plan was supposed to work. However, when AT&T applied for permission to use the manholes, they were denied again. The solution was to enlarge the tunnel to use a small train powered by electricity supplied by overhead wires to bring in cable spools. That was relatively easy given the clay. The tunnel was then covered with a layer of un-reinforced concrete.

In 1903, AT&T renegotiated its contract with the city to expand the tunnels to service the many important businesses directly to their sub-basements. This time the city was more amenable because this would take hundreds of wagons and horses off the city streets.

By 1920, after several bankruptcies, reorganizations, a failed labor strike, and the spending of an estimated $30,000,000, the railroad had expanded its length and its services. Now not only did it bring in retail goods and office supplies, it also began carrying in vast amounts of coal to fire all the boilers and haul out the cinders and trash. At one time (1917) the railroad was using 132 locomotives, 2,000 merchandise cars, 350 excavation cars, and 235 ash and coal cars. Total haulage for the year came to an amazing 552,000 tons.

Service to the downtown sub-basements continued into the 1950s. In the deeper basements, trains simply came in one side of the basement and out the other. In shallower basements sixteen automatic elevators transferred cargo. If the railroad ever operated in the black, it was an exception. The Chicago Tunnel Co. asked for permission from the court to shut down, this time for good. Permission was given and by 1992, the year of the Chicago Flood, only twenty to thirty miles of tunnel were still open.

Some curious facts about the tunnel railroad: It needed no special ventilation system because the trains so filled the tunnel that they pushed fresh air in front of them on the way in and used air on the way out. They had a profitable side business as well. In the days before air conditioning, the constant 55-degree air in the tunnels was pumped to surface structures, particularly theaters in the Chicago summers. When the weather turned cold the same air was usually much warmer than the surface air so it was still pumped up where it took only one third the amount of coal to heat the building.

The city did not completely close access to the tunnel so small groups of unlicensed tours explored them until a terrorist scare in 2000 caused all entrances, even the hidden ones, closed. The tunnel system remains dry, at least for the time being, but continues to be important as electric, fiber optic, and cable television cables run through it

The Chicago Flood of 1992 was a curious one to be sure. How many other cities can claim an invisible flood? One that took no lives, inflicted no injuries, damaged no homes, and caused monetary losses that were measured in the mere millions. It could only happen in Chicago.

16

FIRE ON THE WATER

THE TERRIBLE CRIB DISASTER OF 1909

On a clear day from the beauty of Chicago's lakefront, you can barely make them out with the unaided eye. From a high-rise, with the right view, you'll need some help. They seem so small and far away they might be tricks of the light, a mirage, but they're real as they can be. Too stubby to be lighthouses, they look more like tiny stone fortresses meant to defend some watery realm.

What you're barely seeing is a mystery to many Chicagoans, let alone visitors. They're the remnants of an incredible engineering achievement begun over 150 years ago to serve a quite prosaic purpose, supplying fresh, pure water for the Chicago metropolitan area. Officially they have the name of water intake structures, but by Chicago legend, they have the less than glorious name of "cribs."

The cribs were built from 1865-1935, a period of seven decades. In the construction stages, temporary piers made of fill dredged from the lake floor were topped by wooden structures with slatted sides to protect the workings and crew quarters. From newspaper illustrations, they reminded the still rural-oriented populace of Chicago of nothing so much as corn cribs. For those lacking in agricultural knowledge these ubiquitous wooden structures found on every Midwestern grain farm were used to dry corn before it was sold (The higher the moisture

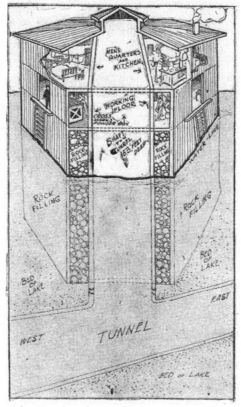

A diagram of a crib structure.

content the lower the price.) A century ago all had slatted wooden sides to promote air circulation.

There were as many as nine cribs built over the years but in 2019 only two, the Dever and Dunne cribs, are still active. One is kept inactive but ready as a back-up. Two have been demolished. Two more are scheduled for demolition and one was built close enough to the original lake shore that it is now surrounded by the acres of landfill added to Lincoln Park. That leaves five sites still to be seen spaced across miles of lakefront. The crib that is the subject of this story, however, is gone for reasons you will soon learn.

The cribs were the most visible evidence of incredibly complex engineering projects, especially when the first was built. One other visible but temporary wonder to behold was an 8000-foot cable suspended from towers capable of carrying crews and supplies between shore and the drilling station. The towers also carried electrical and telephone connections to the cribs.

What couldn't be seen was the most difficult, but vital, part of the marvel. In the case of the crib in question, 160 feet below the lake floor a tunnel was being dug through bedrock to perfectly intersect with a shaft dug vertically from the lake floor beneath the crib. Marvelous precision was needed because both parts of the project were done simultaneously. The intake shaft would eventually pump water from twenty to fifty feet below the lake's surface through mains in the tunnel to the city.

Such extreme measures were needed because contamination from the Chicago River was known to flow out as far as a mile offshore. It's good to remember that the lake shore kept creeping farther into the lake as the years passed, a process which continues. In addition, some way had to be found to protect the water intakes, especially when winter came and the lake water froze.

Until the completion of the John Jardine Filtration Plant in 1968 crews at each crib had to manually keep the intake filters clear of drifting ice, fish bodies, and other debris. Jardine now does this automatically. It easily supplies the daily billion gallons of water taken from the two active cribs to supply the needs of all of Chicago and many of its suburbs.

It's not surprising that in the construction of the earlier cribs the pay and welfare of workers was a low priority. The working conditions were brutal. Heat was oppressive and ventilation and lighting were marginal at best. All workers were provided room and board but the food was unpalatable and unhealthy. Much of the work other than drilling and blasting was done by hand. Injured workers were fired as was anyone who complained. Crews were a combination of experienced hard-rock miners who migrated from job to job and earned perhaps $2.00 per day and unskilled local laborers who were treated even worse for half the pay.

As many as three workers a day used the same bunks. Often company records were shoddily maintained. The only way of identification for illiterate workers was a numbered brass tag they presented to the paymaster for their earnings.

This being Chicago, the presence of graft in the system was rife. If contractors had the right connections and greased the right palms, they could cut corners on wages, materials, maintenance, worker safety, and welfare. Among the violations allowed to exist at the 1909 crib, there were also no sanitation facilities other than a privy. Workers wore the same clothes for their multi-day shift. These two factors alone caused the odor in the crew quarters to be noxious. Storage facilities were in a room connected to the crew quarters and workers reported that gunpowder, dynamite, gasoline, and kerosene were loosely stored while the men nearby smoked. Even the contractor admitted that the only fire-fighting equipment on the crib were some axes and small fire extinguishers. Alcohol was expressly forbidden but the crib was about as dry as the rest of the city anyway. Workers were of many ethnic origins. This made for tensions which, given all the other stresses, caused quarrels and fights to add to the other demoralizing conditions.

The 1909 crib project had been awarded to the general contractor George W. Jackson Co. By the beginning of the year, the construction was well underway. Despite several newspaper exposes of criminal level negligence on the project, nothing changed. There were no failed inspections reported by city departments. Jackson's company was reaping the benefits of its payoffs and, like the failure of due diligence by city officials who declared the Iroquois Theater fireproof six years earlier, opened the door for tragedy.

The Iroquois Theater fire had a combination of circumstances which both increased chances of death and decreased possibilities for survival. Like the earlier fire, winter played a factor, as did overcrowding, inadequate fire-fighting equipment, storage of flammable materials, and available escape routes. The fire broke out early in the morning of January 20. In all, there were at least ninety-six men on the crib, maybe more. Ironically the number of occupants had been increased only a few days prior as it was deemed cost-effective to temporarily house workers from another crib there rather than transfer them to shore.

There was at least one explosion reported when the fire began. It's what alerted boat captains that something was wrong. There may have been other blasts as well. Because the floor was littered with explosives and containers of flammable liquids, it makes sense. All the surrounding walls on both floors were wood so the fire expanded with tragic speed. One man tried to call the shore station for rescue. His words were remembered, "The crib is on fire! For God's sake send help at once or we will be burned alive! The tug . . ." At that, the call ended as the telephone line to shore melted. The overhead trolley which could have saved some men also melted dumping four men who thought they'd been saved into the icy lake waters to drown.

The design of the crib assumed that the only exit needed besides the trolley system would be an opening to load supplies from the company tug, the *T.T. Morford*. There were also a few windows for ventilation big enough for men to squeeze through. Those trapped inside were all helpless. They either suffocated in their bunks or burned to death. Survivors reported hearing screams of the dying and desperate and saw men walking inside with their bodies on fire. The fire did its horrid work in only a few minutes. Not a single survivor was found inside.

Ten feet below the supply port was a scrim of ice which many men were able to jump on. Those fortunate to do so found to their horror they were not safe as the ice crumbled under their weight, plunging them too into the icy lake. Some were able to cling to ice floes, while some even became frozen to them. Those who thus survived drowning had their chances to live diminished by the minutes it took for help to arrive. Small boats who reached the scene first were kept away by the ice. The company tug was at its pier without steam up. Even with frantic work by the crew, it took an hour for her to reach the crib. By then there were few survivors. All of them were suffering from shock and advancing hypothermia. One bearded man was said to have been too weak to grasp a rope which had been repeatedly flung to him. Instead, he allowed himself to slip off his icy raft and sink below the surface.

As with the Iroquois fire, there were few injured. They were taken to Illinois Hospital, treated, and released. As to the numbers of survivors, a total has never been determined. Even worse, the same was true for the number of the dead. The number ranged from forty to seventy depending on the source. There are several reasons for this. One was the destructive nature of the fire. So many bodies were burned so badly or dismembered by explosions that the number of victims was impossible to establish exactly. Another cause was the negligent record-keeping of the Jackson Co. There was no accurate count of those living on the crib at the time. The same negligence applied to identifying the dead. There simply was no reasonably accurate roster of worker names or addresses. Many workers had no permanent address because they floated from one workplace to another. There was little to tell the relatives of those workers who were city residents trying to make a living. And finally, asking to number those who survived the fire only to drown is simply asking too much for 1909.

When the corpses were brought ashore at the company's 92nd St. pier, it was already crowded with thousands seeking news of their loved ones. As the tug *L. C. Sabin* approached another tug, the *Rita McDonald*, brought out Fire Inspector Schuetter and Coroner Peter Hoffman who ordered a delay until the corpses could all be placed in gunny sacks. As the bodies were finally brought to the pier, E.D. Lee, a Jackson traffic manager, raised a hand palm out as he shouted "No newspaper reporters." The cover-up had begun.

All day long the terrified crowd was kept at bay. The Jackson Co. had all the bodies taken to a nearby morgue where police constables half-heartedly kept the crowds out. The company persisted in maintaining it had an accurate list of the number of men on the crib until it was surpassed by the number of bodies brought back. The company refused to release any record it had of workers' names. Reporters were indeed kept away with the aid of company guards. Given this level of resistance, the confusing nature of the events, and the obscurity of the victims, reporters quickly gave up. Many of them were perhaps already thinking that the fix was in and their news stories would be suppressed.

The Jackson Co. was quick to assist in literally burying the disaster or at least its victims. It paid for funerals and allowed a long procession of mourners on city streets. It provided free burial at Mt. Greenwood Cemetery. Today, some without knowledge of the fire, discover the confusing markers of adult victims who were identified listing them as having "died in the crib."

There were immediate outrage and demands for justice. Acting Fire Chief Schuetter claimed, "This is the worst disaster Chicago has known since the Iroquois Theater fire. I will use every man in the department, *if necessary*, to learn who was responsible. The origin of the fire is a mystery. The bodies may never be identified, but we will find out who is to blame!" Coroner Hoffman vowed, "I will impanel a high-class jury and will engage, *if necessary*, experts in mechanics and marine engineering to help me in discovering the responsibility. I do not think there was a dynamite explosion. But the facts have yet to be brought out." (italics are author's) These political appointees even in the heat of the moment were hedging.

To be overly fair these resolves may have been sincere or only to mollify the rage of the mourners, we'll never know. What we do know is that Chicago fathers wanted to cover up a major scandal involving an enormously expensive and highly touted civic engineering project, a clout-heavy contractor, and complicity by city employees. Any honest investigation could go all the way to the top and result in the firing of many city workers and resignations of politicians. It should be expected then that there was never an inquiry of any sort, thus no culpability was found and no one was punished. The most that can be hoped is that some consciences may have been bothered for a long time.

Because there were no investigations, an immediate cause for the fire will never be established. One survivor claimed that a worker had soaked his and others' mattresses with gasoline to treat their bed-bug ridden bunks. Another blamed the careless discarding of still-burning pipe ashes. Most of the survivors interviewed mentioned the careless storage of gunpowder and dynamite sticks rolling across the floor.

Nearly half-way between the other two great early twentieth Century Chicago disasters, the Iroquois theater fire of 1903 and the sinking of the SS *Eastland* in 1915, the crib fire of 1909 pales by comparison in loss of life, but not in terror. Even more than the surviving cribs, it has become one of Chicago's greatest mysteries.

17

CHICAGO ON THE AIR

EARLY CHICAGO RADIO AND TELEVISION

Radio broadcasting in Chicago began as it did in cities across America in the early 1920s. By then the wireless transmission of sound was well established. The prime example was still the distress signals from the RMS *Titanic* to shore stations and other ships at sea. Though these were Morse Code, not voice messages, the concept was very similar; the signals broke an electric current in a predictable pattern and sent it through the air to a receiver tuned to the same frequency. It was telegraph without the poles and wires. The English connect it so closely with voice radio that to this day radio is called "wireless" there.

After the restrictions of WWI ended, entrepreneurs began to think of ways to make a new concept make money. Chicago was just one of many American cities to follow the success of KDKA in Pittsburg in finding the right combination of transmitters and receivers to send voice messages to nearby private homes. You could call this invention telephone without the poles or wires. There were several major problems at first. Transmitters and receivers were both limited in power and existed only in small numbers. Those who owned the receivers were building them themselves as experiments or hobbies. Reception was by line-of-sight, meaning that any tall building or hill would block the signal. So could atmospheric conditions. On both transmitting stations and in homes, an outside antenna was needed, the taller the better.

A lot of large-scale research and development was necessary and someone needed to pay for it. At the time, Americans were dependent on the print medium for their news, opinion, and even their product information so it was logical that every city had more than one major newspaper. The publishers of these not only had deep pockets but the vision to see the potential of radio as competition and a chance to control it. Similarly, since radio was an electrical medium, large corporations like Commonwealth Edison and Westinghouse were interested. Another source was wealthy individual investors who saw potential in the new medium.

This is a point where the United Kingdom and the United States fundamentally split on developmental strategies. In the more socialistic UK, the development, sponsorship, and programming were all nationalized into the BBC. In the US all of these were done privately. The federal government had no jurisdiction nor desire to take over.

There were also many questions about how to use the new technology to make a profit. How could you get those people who were so used to getting nearly all information through their eyes to become listeners to sound coming out of a box other than a phonograph or telephone? And how did you bring the cost down so that the radio wasn't just another toy of the rich? When the first autos were assembled, they were often few and hand-built which made them expensive to buy, operate, and repair. Radio receivers at first were the same. They were hand-built in factories and installed in expensive cabinetry to compliment the rest of the furnishings in a gracious home.

This made the decision of what to broadcast on the first Chicago radio station, KYW, a bit easier. For the first year, the only programs on the station were live broadcasts of Chicago Grand Opera Company performances. Socialites would invite their friends to their homes for afternoon or evening listening to the fascinating new phenomenon. This was surely of limited appeal, but the statistics show that when the 1923 season began there were 200 radio sets in Chicago. By the end of the opera season, the number had grown to 25,000.

This rapid expansion of popularity became a problem when the airwaves in the city were soon crowded by more than twenty stations unregulated in programming, transmitter power, and frequencies. Stations played on top of others. They changed their call letters, owners, and formats and came and went without warning. None of them could come close to filling a twenty-four-hour broadcast day.

Until technology brought down the cost and raised the reliability of radio, programming was decided and sponsors could be shown the efficacy of the new medium, private support was necessary. WMAQ was supported by the *Chicago Daily News*. Another great paper, the *Chicago Tribune* supported WGN, a station to promote its slogan "World's Greatest Newspaper." WBBM was carried by the wealthy brothers Les and Ralph Atlass in partnership with Stewart Warner. Sears Roebuck & Co. also used its slogan "World's Largest Store" in the call letters of the station it owned, WLS. WCFL was similarly owned and funded by the Chicago Federation of Labor and WMBI by the Moody Bible Institute. WCRW, WEDC, and WSBC existed to broadcast in the languages of some of Chicago's ethnic communities.

While all of this was happening, radio was mimicking the success of Henry Ford's Model T. By the late 20s and early 30s, millions of sets had been sold across the country as they became more portable, inexpensive, and standardized for easy repair. City sets were most often run on AC power from home electricity. Great numbers of DC-powered sets were sold in the country to customers who had no electricity. In these areas, the radio depended on the Model T or other vehicles. The battery used to start the engine could be brought inside the house to power the radio set then returned to the car for recharging. This brought a major change to at least one station in Chicago—WLS. Sears & Roebuck wanted to establish a better class of clientele than farmers even though it annually made tens of millions of dollars from them in mail-order sales. In 1928 it sold WLS to a very popular agrarian magazine named *Prairie Farmer*. It kept the program which most embarrassed Sears. The "WLS Barn Dance" perpetuated one the longest running types of programming in radio and broadcast history. The old Barn Dance format can still be experienced by listening to *Grand Ol' Opry* from Nashville.

Between 1926 and 1934, the federal government struggled to find ways to organize and regulate the chaotic new medium. Courts had twice struck down any attempt to control licensing under the Interstate Commerce Act, so stations proliferated, adding to the confusion. Finally things became so bad Congress created legislation to bring order. New licenses were limited and frequencies were assigned along with call letters. (The rule became that stations east of the Mississippi must have call letters beginning with "W," and west of the river with "K." For the most part stations were allowed to keep the call letters they already had. Thus the pioneering station in Pittsburg, KDKA, retains its historic identity.) Transmitter power and locations were also regulated.

During this period and partially due to the growing predictability brought by the newly established Federal Radio Commission, (FRC, later FCC) stations began to consolidate into two powerful networks, the Columbia Broadcasting System (CBS) and the National Broadcasting Corporation (NBC). NBC eventually became so large it split into smaller Red and Blue Networks. The advantages of networks were the same as business mergers have always been. Costs were brought down by reducing redundant programming, staffs, casts, studios, and transmission facilities. Networks could afford to locate their antennae on the top of the tallest skyscrapers or the highest hilltops around. Concentration also made it possible for networks to carry unsponsored programming referred to as "sustaining" to fill the broadcast day of eighteen hours they had pledged the FRC. Sustaining programs were vital to prevent so-called "dead air," a time when no program was being sent out. Listeners were likely to change stations and not likely to return.

By 1928, AT&T had stretched its transmission lines to the Pacific Coast. This meant New York City studios could not create enough programming for the broadcast day. There were simply not enough voice actors available because all programming was done live. As a direct result, Chicago entered its brief Golden Age. Some of the most popular radio shows came from the Windy City. Many historians list Chicago-based *Amos 'n Andy* as the most popular radio show of all time. (There's an urban legend that you could walk down a neighborhood street and not miss a minute of Amos 'n Andy because you could hear the show from every front porch or open window.) Another show always found in the top ten in ratings was *Fibber McGee & Molly* featuring Jim and Marion Jordan, former vaudevillians from nearby Peoria, Illinois. Two of the most popular children's shows, serials starring *Little Orphan Annie* and *Jack Armstrong, All-American Boy* aired from Chicago.

These and other Chicago shows were mixed with New York shows during what came to be called evening "prime time." Pure Chicago-based programming was pretty much limited to the morning and early afternoon. The primary example would be Don McNeil's *Breakfast Club* which aired for an incredible thirty-five years. Its popularity was so great it became a national show as did the WLS *Barn Dance*. Noon times and afternoons were at least partially devoted to children's programming. One Chicago morning experiment was the talk show. Dave Garroway began as a morning host for *Garroway at Large* which in the early 50s became the NBC network *Today* show. Garroway was the host for the first nine years.

The rest of the Chicago broadcast day before prime-time was dominated by the Chicago originated format known as "soap operas," so called because they were usually sponsored by advertising aimed at the home-maker, the controller of the purse strings in nearly all family spending. "Soaps" then were the same as they are now, little dramas of everyday life with familiar characters, plots, and situations which never did seem to get resolved. It's an amazing fact that nearly all of the soaps were created, directed, and produced by only three people. Irna Phillips was responsible for dozens over the years. Anne and Frank Hummert similarly cranked out as many as ninety fifteen-minute weekday segments from their stable of writers, actors, and staffs. Since they were never seen, actors could be totally unlike the character they played and could appear on several different shows on the same day or as different characters on the same show. Many of the Chicago-based soaps were picked up for national broadcast and some of them easily transferred to television.

Each of the major networks had a prestigious building for its Chicago headquarters and studios. CBS was in the Wrigley Building, NBC in the

Merchandise Mart, and upstart Mutual in the Tribune Tower. As their dominance decreased, lesser stations found less luxurious accommodations. There they filled their mornings with local personalities and their afternoons with kids' programming and syndicated programs in the evening. (Syndicated programs were produced by independent studios and sold to local and sometimes network stations. Today excellent examples of syndicated shows are *Jeopardy* and *Wheel of Fortune*.) You had to use a radio guide to find them on the dial as they would be on different nights and hours and have local sponsors. While some of the stations would shut down for late evening and early morning hours, others would broadcast remote pick-ups of small combos or Big Bands from downtown Chicago's most important ballrooms, hotel lounges, restaurants, and night clubs. Remotes were symbiotic. The hotel and band did not charge in return for the publicity.

Chicago's decline as a major broadcast center was postponed by a WWII delay in the laying of a coaxial cable to Los Angeles. When it finally did reach the Pacific in 1949, things changed rapidly. Network operations including programs were shifted to LA or Hollywood. Mostly soaps and some local productions were left.

With the elimination of all that network programming and the rise of FM technology, Chicago radio underwent a fundamental change. Nearly all music from pop to classical moved to the FM band. Only when Rock 'n Roll appeared did some stations like WLS-AM make themselves over to appeal to teenagers who not only loved the music but the teams of DJs as well. AM made the music much more available to the young audience through their car and home radios. The rest of the AM dial became the home of talk, news, and sports radio. Other stations played lush, easy listening music hosted by soothing, sophisticated DJs such as Franklyn MacCormack and John Doremus in all night programming.

The early end of Chicago's importance in radio gave it a leg up in pioneering television. While New York and LA/Hollywood also had facilities for powerful and artful broadcasting they were still well involved in radio because it remained a profit-making business. The networks' approach to television was to put it off to the future and see what happened with radio. NBC particularly snubbed television development. Young technicians, engineers, and those others with a vision for the new medium were not encouraged. They were attracted to the Chicago market where pioneering television was gaining traction. The basics of television had been achieved by the early '40s but were suspended for the war. TV was seen once again as a rich person's toy, not nearly as important as other scientific developments like radar, sonar, and computer-assisted weaponry.

After the war, it was therefore only a matter of how to use the new medium. What type of programming would be successful? How were these programs to be broadcast? Who would pay for them? Not surprisingly, nearly all of the first television formatting came straight from the radio. There were local quiz shows, news, and commentary. These familiar shows evolved quickly on Chicago TV. For example, news always spent much more time on the weather. Long before the advent of radar and satellite-aided forecasting, green screens, and graphics, weather forecasts were both longer and more entertaining on TV than radio even though for years they featured only a person in front of a weather map with a pointer and some symbols for clouds and sunshine, perhaps some showers, winds and snowflakes as well. Weather reporters were not always meteorologists. Two of the most popular were Clint Youle, who had a meteorology degree, while P.J. Hoff had been an editorial cartoonist in a previous life.

News continued to cover the globe but local and regional stories generated better ratings. Instead of network analysts such as H.V. Kaltenborn there were no-frills, actual print reporters who did their own investigating and writing. They read their editorials from cue cards, not teleprompters and tablets. Two of the most popular were Clifton Utley, Sr and Len O'Connor. The latter took delight in skewering his fellow Chicago Irishman, Richard J. Daly. Much to the mayor's anger, O'Connor referred to him as "Boss" Daly.

Children's programming had always been especially well done in Chicago. That was continued between "school's out" and "supper's on." Some of the most popular and highly acclaimed children's programs in history came out of Chicago. To be sure there were lesser lights such as *Elmer the Elephant* with the radio re-tread John Conrad, but they were still lots of fun for the kiddies. But, consider *Kukla, Fran, and Ollie* created by Burr Tilstrom on WMAQ. It was quickly picked up by national television. Surveys showed that as many adults watched it as children. Its simple plots and friendly, funny characters were pleasing to everybody. The program was awarded two Emmys and a Peabody Award. In a similar format, many kids' favorite show was *Garfield Goose and Friends*.

It would be a serious omission to leave the subject of Chicago children's programs without mentioning *Bozo's Circus*. It, too, attracted viewers of all ages and lasted for a long time as well. The circus ringmaster was Ned Locke, another WGN radio kid's specialist. This ringmaster was the straight man, however. Much more memorable was Bozo the Clown, who played all the tricks. *The Bozo Show* was so popular that couples

Kukla Fran and Ollie (Courtesy of the Wikimedia Commons public domain.)

bought tickets before they had children because waiting time for this live audience show was measured in years.

For years Sunday mornings were reserved for religious programs including remote services from area churches and evening choir performances. Saturday and Sunday afternoons studios might cover baseball or football games both college and professional. In addition, there might be re-runs of old films. "B" cowboy movies were especially popular with children and bred heroes and heroines like Gene Autry, Roy Rogers, Dale Evans, and Annie Oakley, all of whom got their own television shows. On weekend evenings, different kinds of sports gained popularity for the first time. Professional wrestling and prizefighting filled the small screen and stadiums as well. During baseball season, Cubs and White Sox home games were televised with legendary announcers Jack Brickhouse for the Cubs and Bob Elson for the White Sox.

As CBS, NBC, Mutual, and the brand-new ABC caught up with television development Chicago prime-time programming became increasingly network oriented.

Over the years the rights to old Hollywood films, good, bad, and in between were purchased and packaged. Again stealing a format from radio where shows like *Lux Radio Theater* and *Screen Guild Players* presented condensed versions of great films usually starring the original actors. Complete, classic films came to home television. New generations were introduced to masters like Laurel and Hardy, Andy Hardy, and hundreds of others. Youngsters were able to stay at home and wonder at the splendor of *Gone with the Wind* and join the fantasy of *The Wizard of Oz* right beside their parents.

Chicago pioneered in yet another broadcast genre when in 1955 WTTW-TV became the first and most-watched public television station in the nation. In this case, the call letters were for Chicago's *Window To The World.* Instead of a subsidy from the federal government, the station was created with funds from Edward Ryerson of Ryerson Steel combined with other private funding. At first, WTTW concentrated on educational classes for adults. Later it changed its morning focus to children's programming namely *Sesame Street* and *Electric Company.* Evenings were still for adults with fine arts simulcasts with WFMT-FM radio, its sister station. It also found success in giving American audiences the chance to see BBC programming on *Masterpiece Theater* and similar shows.

By 1970, Chicago was pioneering yet another TV genre, the talk show, beginning with Phil Donahue and progressing to its peak with Oprah Winfrey. Some other programs which originated in Chicago were the lower quality *Jenny McCarthy* and *Jerry Springer Shows*.

Television in Chicago and elsewhere was undeniably a beneficiary of the development of radio. When it was ready to boom the infrastructure was already in place in the form of studios and other broadcast facilities. Hundreds of experienced radio actors and staff members meant television had its pick of the best. Ready and willing to switch was an audience of millions of radio listeners and dozens of willing sponsors. As noted earlier, nearly all of early television and much of it today came from similar formats on the radio. Stars of radio made conversions to early television as well. All of this meant that television didn't have to re-invent the wheel. It soon ended the concept of nation-wide radio as it had been and replaced it via satellite radio with literally hundreds of shows available. Technological progress has brought broadcasting to us in ever more varied formats and convenient devices. In 2019 the dominance of the visual is almost complete.

18

THE *PRAIRIE FARMER* STATION

THE WLS NATIONAL BARN DANCE

Long forgotten and obscured by the changes in American society, there once was a legendary radio show coming out of Chicago that for decades was the most popular in much of the nation. Perhaps forgotten because of its simple, old-fashioned format, or perhaps obscured by conflation with the "Grand Ole Opry," the WLS *National Barn Dance* is now remembered only by the oldest Midwesterners. Even the histories of the Golden Age of Radio seem to have lost knowledge of this original country music broadcast.

In the wide-open days of early commercial radio when programs, ownership, and call letters could change daily, everything was in flux. There were no rules or precedents to follow. Broadcasting cost a lot so most stations were owned by businesses who were, by and large, unsure of the potential for such an acquisition, but didn't want to be left behind.

One of these companies with deep pockets was Sears, Roebuck & Co. It funded a station modestly named for its huge mail-order store on Homan Ave. WLS stands for World's Largest Store, to leave no doubt in listeners' minds of the company's importance. WLS had a transmitter powerful enough to reach most of the Midwest and at night thirty-eight of the forty-eight states. This coverage did make it the closest thing there was at the time to a national station.

Sears had, of course, achieved fame and immense fortune by the development of its catalog retail business which shipped orders literally around the world from Chicago. By the early '20s, the company was beginning a major shift from mail-order to brick and mortar stores in urban areas. Executives thought that a sophisticated new radio station, the latest wonder in technology, would help the customer base switch from catalogs to in-store shopping.

In the early, learning years, station executives were often the same as those that controlled the business. Since there were no experienced radio managers around yet, they turned programming over to their retail managers. So there was no second thought to giving management of WLS to Edgar Bill and Farm Director Samuel Guard. They were instructed to fill the broadcast day with classical music, opera, and lectures.

Bill had been with Sears for some time and like many of its other executives had been born and raised in the country. He remembered the impromptu nature of Saturday night, home-made entertainment literally held in a barn—the largest space available. It would be a good guess that the classical format bored him stiff. In fact, Bill later remarked, "We had so much highbrow music the first week that we thought it would be a good idea to get on some of the old-time music." He realized something the self-styled sophisticates running Sears didn't. Chicago, while being prosperous, progressive, and populous wasn't the same in terms of culture as eastern cities such as Boston, Philadelphia, and New York City and it would be some time, if ever before the "toddlin town" caught up. Further, Bill was enough of a prescient retailer to realize that Chicago was surrounded for hundreds of miles in every direction by farms and tens of millions of rural residents. He also knew Chicago itself was full of residents who might have possessed a big city address but still had rural roots.

By April 19, 1924, the first Saturday night after WLS signed on the air, *National Barn Dance* began. Somehow Bill had organized a two-hour performance by quickly gathering enough available, if not all polished, acts to fill the time slot. At first, the performers were barely above local, amateur talent. Those who get the credit for the earliest shows included

Tony Dandurand, Tom Owens, Pie Plant Pete, Chubby Parker, Cecil and Ethel, and Rube Transon.

Predictably, Sears executives were appalled that this "disgraceful low-brow show" was on the station they hoped would help the company seem less rural rather than pandering to the country folk. Bill and Guard were immediately called into a meeting to explain their treachery. The two were prepared and only had to show the baskets of congratulatory letters, telegrams, and records of phone calls for the new program to quell the officers' anger, at least for a while.

As its fame and budget increased, so did its staff and the quality of its performers. One staff member who was lost was George D. Hay, who fashioned himself as "The Solemn Old Judge." He was stolen away by WSM in Nashville, who wanted to duplicate the *National Barn Dance* format. Hayes did help WSM with the beginnings of what would become in a few years the *Grand Ole Opry*. He also helped himself to a false claim that he was the one who created *National Barn Dance*.

If *National Barn Dance* was given short shrift by radio historians, they were missing the fact that some of the biggest acts in radio and television cut their teeth on the show. In the late '20s, two White comics, Freeman Gosden and Charles Correll, wrote and performed a show they named *Sam 'n Henry*. A dispute with management caused them to leave WLS and appear only a week later on the Chicago NBC affiliate, WMAQ. In doing so, they had to change the name of the act to *Amos 'n Andy*. This gentle and funny, yet intelligent show became arguably the most popular radio show in history and lasted another thirty years.

Near the same time, Jim and Marion Jordan, whose home was just ninety miles from Chicago in Peoria, IL, broke in an act named "The Smith Family." They, too, soon left for WMAQ where after some fine tuning became *Fibber McGee & Molly*, another radio legend. These defections were not surprising as neither fit the true National Barn Dance philosophy. "Sam 'n Henry" were two "Black" men who defied the stereotypes of the age by showing their characters as ordinary men with the same problems everyone had. They were much more accepted by urban listeners, and the Jordans could certainly see they were not going to make their act change and grow by staying on WLS.

In 1928, some changes occurred which were responsible for a great expansion of *National Barn Dance's* success. Sears and Roebuck realized that its radio tool for achieving a change of the firm's orientation from farm to city was hopelessly lost to a rural audience. For a token amount they sold the station to a popular Chicago-based magazine, *The Prairie Farmer*. From then until 1960, WLS was known as "The Prairie Farmer Station." All of its programming was tuned to the agricultural audience.

The owner and publisher of the magazine was Burridge Butler, who not only depended on rural life for the success of his business but personified the moral values of that life. He instituted a strict code of conduct for his new employees. Very few had any qualms about the moral code because it was in sync with how they were raised and what they had come to believe. Most of them stayed put. They became so close to each other over the years they considered themselves a family, sharing each other's joys and tragedies. The cast members adopted the name "Haylofters" for themselves.

Despite the bargain price, Burridge Butler took on a significant debt when he bought WLS. *Barn Dance* alone regularly had a payroll of one hundred. This did not include local square dance groups who would voluntarily travel hundreds of miles and pay their own expenses to dance to the show's famous callers and square dance musicians. Stars of the show were coming at a higher price. Just a few of the enduring stalwarts and visiting acts were Lulu Belle and Scotty, Arkie the Arkansas Woodchopper, the Dezurick Sisters and the Dinning Sisters, the Hoosier Hot Shots, and Cpt. Stubby and the Buccaneers, a sort of less slick Spike Jones group, if that is even possible. The show had several announcers, but the best known is Joe Kelly. He was a man of limited talent and would tell you so. He played the rather slow-witted, bemused foil on *Barn Dance* as he did on his other show *The Quiz Kids* on which he regularly and genuinely reacted with befuddlement at the erudition of the show's precocious prodigies.

Lula Belle and Scotty from the WLS Barn Dance.

Some country stars were not regular members of the Haylofters but appeared frequently on both *Barn Dance* and *Grand Ole Opry* as they toured the country. Two of them were comedians who went on to success in other media. For example, little "Lonesome George" Gobel was later the star of his own television program. Pat Buttram was a regular on *Barn Dance*. He found he could make people laugh in films and on television if he found the right side-kick part.

By far the most famous name coming out of the show was Gene Autry. Autry became a star of dozens of "B" movie westerns in which he never got to marry the girl but always managed to get in a few songs. He increased his success as the star of radio and television shows bearing his name. Loyally, even after achieving this greater fame, he came back from time-to-time to perform with his friends on *Barn Dance*.

In 1931, the show's expense caused Butler and his fellow executives to make two risky decisions. They would move the program from the small WLS radio theater to the 1200-seat Eighth Street Theater and charge admission. Their decisions immediately proved wise. Audience members didn't complain about the ticket prices. In fact, tickets were sold out a month in advance. Crowds would line up for blocks even though they all had reserved seats. There was a performance at 7:30 for those east of the Mississippi and a second show at 10:00 for those in the rest of the country, each with a separate audience. With all those sold-out shows and twenty-six years in the Eighth St. Theater, WLS figured almost three million people saw the show live. Butler needn't have worried about funding, for two more benefits of the show's immense popularity came quickly. In 1932, NBC put Barn Dance on its Blue network. Thirty more stations now carried the show and because it was now truly national, it gained a big-name underwriter, Miles Laboratories—the makers of Alka Seltzer, which also sponsored *The Quiz Kids*.

All radio shows had a summer hiatus. During these stifling months, the Haylofters would take the show on the road, playing at the largest state fairs. Though the logistics and staging of a roadshow were challenging, the performances were wonderful and attracted great crowds who would wait in line for hours for a chance to see their idols in person.

In 1944, *Barn Dance* reached another milestone of recognition. A Hollywood movie was made creatively titled *The National Barn Dance*. The plot is simplistic, a variant on the theme "Let's Give A Show." It's a film about making a radio show. A Chicago advertising agent wants to put together a radio program with "hillbilly" acts. He accidentally and coincidentally finds just what he is looking for in a barn on a Saturday night somewhere in downstate Illinois where he is mesmerized by the merry-making music and comedy. The group of amateurs agrees to all go together to Chicago for the show. This film was about as unsophisticated as *Barn Dance* itself, so it was at least a fair conception. Many of the *Barn*

Dance regulars perform in the film including Pat Buttram, the Hoosier Hot Shots, Lulu Belle, and Scotty and Joe Kelly.

Barn Dance stayed on NBC until 1946 when it switched to ABC. ABC-TV did a thirty-nine-week season of televised *Barn Dance* programs, but the series ended there. ABC ended its affiliation in 1952 because the show was waning in the polls. Something needed to be done. *Grand Ole Opry* had already switched from true country music to "honky-tonk," Country-Western, and eventually "rockabilly" music. That worked. Burridge Butler again risked all by vowing to stay true to his program's country foundations. Most of the performers agreed. As a result, the show continued "pure," but now was heard only on WLS-AM radio. Remember this was a 50,000-watt signal so it was still "national" in scope.

Midwest culture had changed quickly in the preceding decade. Now family farmers were getting university degrees and finding in their wider experiences an embarrassment for true country music as "hick" and old-fashioned. The Chicago audience was by now also much more sophisticated in its tastes and only lightly connected to country customs. The Eighth St. Theater was no longer filled; so, to cut costs, in 1956 a decision was made ending audience viewing.

In 1959 ABC bought WLS's desirable central spot on the AM dial and its powerful transmission facilities. There was no money in *Barn Dance* anymore so WLS-AM became a haven for teens who loved its Top 40/Rock 'n Roll playlist and its stable of hip, wise-cracking, irreverent disc jockeys. Despairingly for older folks, the special entertainment they had for decades enjoyed on *Barn Dance* was now replaced by that "devil's music." There were enough of those concerned, conservative listeners for *Barn Dance* to be continued on one of the most conservative, not to say reactionary, American stations, Col. Robert McCormick's Chicago Tribune flagship, WGN. Even there it was apparent that *Barn Dance* loyalists were aging and rapidly declining in numbers. The American icon left the air for good in 1968 after an incredible run of forty-four years, almost two generations.

There is no doubt that the WLS *National Barn Dance* was the pioneer of all broadcast country music and entertainment shows. There is no criticism to be made of WSM unless it claims to be the original country music station. In appropriating the Barn Dance model, *Grand Ole Opry* is demonstrating that, after all, "Imitation is the sincerest form of flattery." It's also worthy of mentioning that rather than abandon their original beliefs Burridge Butler and the *Barn Dance* gang put their values above popularity or even survival.

19

THE WINDY CITY'S MUSICAL GIFT TO THE WORLD

CHICAGO STYLE BLUES

To say we have the "blues" in life means we feel sad, depressed, lonely, afraid, beaten-down, disappointed, jilted, or crushed by what life has brought us. Blues music is that emotion expressed by means of musical voice and instrumentation.

Break blues music down to its elements and you'll find a series of progressive guitar chords and flattened minor notes on the scale. The original instrumentation of blues was the acoustic guitar and the harmonica or "blues harp." It is uncomplicated music, easy to learn to play, but hard to play right. And the emotion even harder to master. The fact is that though they play together and listen and learn from each other, no two bluesmen play the blues exactly the same way. It is unique to the musician.

Nearly all Americans have some common knowledge of the origins of the blues. They're common with the origins of jazz. The foundations were chants, hollers, rhythms, and beats which were found amongst African peoples who had been sold into slavery in America. They were used to maintain pride, identity, connections to others, and coded messages of complaint and escape.

By the end of the nineteenth century, so-called "slave music" had blended with the gospel music sung in Black churches to form the earliest blues. Blues music was thus almost exclusively Black music. Few Whites had the perspective or memories to feel it. The oldest blues came from the rural Mississippi Delta and was spread in delta cities such as New Orleans and Biloxi.

Constants of blues became apparent from its roots. First, it would always be evolving and as varied as the bluesmen who played it. Second, blues, like its counterpart jazz was uniquely American. There was nothing else like it in the world. Bluesman learned a bit from each musical style they heard played wherever they were. They adopted a bit from classical music, parlor music, and more as they encountered it. They learned from music they heard in clubs, auditoriums, and on street corners. They adopted what pleased them. This was at once the cause and the effect of blues improvisational nature and that the old bluesmen never copied their music out nor composed it. Almost none knew how to read music and, in fact, most of them couldn't read at all.

From the delta, blues moved up-river as the bluesmen found employment on riverboats or the limited employment they could find in day jobs in the increasingly Jim Crow South after Reconstruction. The next center for blues came to be Memphis where the blues stayed long enough to form a new style—Memphis Blues. The Memphis sound wavered from the individual player to so-called "jug bands" which emphasized danceable, syncopated, up-tempo music played on multiple instruments including homemade violins, pianos, the kazoo, and the signature earthen jugs. It was meant not only to enjoy music for themselves but to be hired by privileged Whites to play their now more understandable "darky music." Here trained Black musicians begin to compose music which attempted to capture blues on paper. The most famous is a classic blues composition called "The Memphis Blues" by W.C. Handy.

The next big city north on the Mississippi was St. Louis. Here there was already a rich mixture of musical styles popular before the blues arrived. Once again the blues evolved to include them and change. It was in St. Louis that W.C. Handy published what is the greatest blues song ever, "The St. Louis Blues" in 1914. And in case you didn't know it or make the connection, the St. Louis National Hockey League team is named the St. Louis Blues to cash in on the fame.

It was in St. Louis too that blues encountered a brand-new style of music sweeping the nation, ragtime. Its best-known composer, Scott Joplin lived in St. Louis from 1901-1907. Ragtime exploded in popularity at the time of the fabulous Lewis and Clark Centennial Exhibition or "St. Louis World's Fair" in 1903. It was a special, optimistic age for Americans voiced by the song lyrics. "Meet me in St. Louis, Louie, meet me at the fair. Don't tell me the lights are shining anywhere but there," even if they did come from a 1944 Hollywood musical.

The evolution of Chicago as a blues city with its own recognizable style began in a similar pattern to that in Memphis and St. Louis with some important differences. The first was that the arrival of blues in Chicago had no connection to the Mississippi River. Second, it wasn't a gradual infiltration of small numbers of musicians wandering in. And finally, in Chicago bluesmen found no local or regional music traditions to adapt to or adopt.

The arrival of bluesmen in Chicago came as part of the mass exodus of Black citizen fleeing the increasingly oppressive and dangerous Jim Crow South after WWI which came to be called The Great Migration. Whole families came hoping to find better opportunities for work in the industrial centers of the north such as Chicago and Detroit. Also different about the great movement was that it was nearly all done on railroads like the Illinois Central which ran on a direct New Orleans-Chicago line. Despite the segregated passenger cars, it was preferred because it was safer and quicker than road travel.

Once here, there was still much to help fuel the blues as life in the north proved almost as racist, segregated, and restrictive as it was back in the South. Whether it came to housing, travel, education, medical care recreation, and general safety, racism was everywhere. In 1919, a race riot which began when a young black man was accidentally carried by currents into the "Whites Only" beach. He was beaten and stoned to death on the spot. In the resulting rioting, fourteen Whites and twenty-three

Blues street musicians.

Blacks were killed and about one thousand Black families were made homeless when their homes were burned by White mobs.

Musicians arrived with the tide of The Great Migration and found a barren ground. There were few, in any clubs with knowledge of blues. Segregation restricted those to a small area of the Near South Side within Bronzeville and a few clubs on the West, so blues was often played at noisy rent parties, house parties, rowdy bars, or on street corners such as those in the internationally famous melting pot known as Maxwell Street.

These appearances which made the music harder to hear was the incubator for Chicago style blues. It was easier to make the music louder than to make the audiences quieter. To accomplish this, guitars were miked, amps added, and the beat allowed to take a greater harshness in the blues. Bluesmen and musicologists, in general, referred to the new style as "urban" or "industrial" blues, a style that was harder-edged and angrier and more cynical than its predecessors.

In the 1930s and through WWII, blues audiences remained almost exclusively Black. White people still didn't get it and they found it undanceable unlike Big Band music. It wasn't pop music either or the jazz or Dixieland that they liked better. They called it "race music," not that the bluesmen cared.

After the War, Americans in general, White people perhaps more than ever, remembered the deprivation of the Depression and the sacrifices of war similar to what Black people have always experienced. White people found themselves a bit more cynical and a lot more open to new ideas. They began to discover blues music for the first time. Soon larger and more permanent clubs opened and blues was now not only accepted, it was the "best new thing" among the young who wanted to consider themselves "hip."

As the blues became more legitimate and their music more popular, bluesmen were soon able to do something they'd never done before: make a living at playing. They could get extended "gigs" at clubs and move from one club to another and still find a paying audience with an ever-higher cover charge. Clubs became more crowded and the sight of waiting lines familiar.

The next logical step in the progression of Chicago style blues may not have been the first or even second thing on the minds of the bluesmen, but expanding the cash flow by recording Chicago Blues easily occurred to those in the record business. Because of racial prejudice, it was possible for bluesmen to find recording contracts with only Black-owned studios. It also meant a change to the impromptu nature of the style. To be recorded in a studio, the music needed to be written. There were already a few studios in the business and they hired producers and engineers to increase the output. One recording company, Chess, stands out far above the rest. With its fabled producer Willie Dixon, it recorded thousands of songs by hundreds of artists from 1950-69. Cobra, Delmar, and Alligator were Black-oriented studios as well. Chicago-based musicians made the bulk of the recordings, but blues masters of any style touring the clubs were likely to find a way to one of the recording studios while they were in town. By the 1970s Chicago Blues was so established that the major labels, Paramount, RCA Victor, and Columbia co-opted the style and were marketing it.

Chicago Blues had finally achieved mainstream acceptance. And what an acceptance it was! Since 1984, the Chicago Blues Festival has been the most popular of the Grant Park giant music festivals. It can draw 650,000 fans in a three-day show. If that doesn't make it Chicago's official music there is something dreadfully wrong.

But is that a good thing or a bad thing? Certainly it's a good thing for the true bluesman who had struggled with making a living. But if it leads to formulaic blues playing it would be the antithesis of the reason for blues in the first place. There is a sort of compromise. If you are a true aficionado you know where to find the originals. If you only want an entertaining evening out you can go somewhere more comfortable.

There is a crucial extra dimension for Chicago style blues which must be mentioned. The basic musicality of blues styles and the driving force of Chicago style blues, in particular, has influenced every other style of popular music in the last sixty years. Willie Dixon at Chess recorded and promoted Chuck Berry and Bo Diddly. Proponents of the style Howlin' Wolf, Big Bill Broonzy, Mighty Joe Young, Billy Boy Arnold, and Buddy Guy have all been credited with great influence by groups as powerful as the Beatles and Led Zeppelin. Both have credited recordings they repeatedly listened to in England with influencing their style. There is no coincidence that one of Muddy Waters most well-known songs was "Rolling Stone." The Stones don't think so. It wasn't rare for Mick Jagger and Robert Plant to show up at clubs to jam with Chicago bluesman. Musician Sugar Blue states, "Country, hip-hop, rock 'n roll, funk if you take the blues out all of the (sic) none of this music exist (sic)."

It would be good to know if the blues of Chicago is still alive and well. It is. It's found all over the city and suburbs now. Lists of favorite clubs often appear to suggest the best spots to take it in. If you're in Chicago look for Rosa's Lounge, Kingston Mills, and the appropriately named B.L.U.E.S. on the North Side and Lee's Unleaded Blues, The New Checkerboard Lounge, and Buddy Guy's Legends on the South Side. These are all well-established legitimate showcases where you'll find the best of the blues at a hefty cost. If you want the newest of the blues, the evolving blues, you will have to dig deeper.

20

BUILDING THE IKE

CONSTRUCTION OF THE EISENHOWER EXPRESSWAY

If the Chicago east-west crosstown superhighway wasn't the first one built, it was the first one planned. As far back as 1909, a "grand axis" was designed as part of his Plan for Chicago by Daniel Burnham. He saw it as making a triumphal entry and exit from the Loop and lakefront. It would leave Grant Park on Congress Parkway as a grand boulevard toward a shiny new civic center.

Though Burnham's plan has been a powerful directive for the growth of Chicago which gave us the beautiful city core it enjoys today, the civic center was never built. Neither was the grand boulevard, but the concept of a grand axis was remembered by generations of city planners.

As early as the late 1920s, auto and truck traffic were clogging city streets. Chicago's position at the south end of Lake Michigan and its center position of America's rail network meant a lot of commerce had to be carried. By the 1930s, trucks had been so improved in efficiency and reliability that they became practical to enter interstate travel hauling freight in ways the railroads could never duplicate. Traffic delays increased simply because all that interstate travel had to use city streets to get through and around Chicago. In 1927 the Chicago Plan Commission laid out a system of multi-lane, limited access highways radiating from the Loop. The first of these was experimental, named Lake Shore Drive. It was carefully designed with the multi-lanes, limited access, and diamond exchanges which met the requirements of the original plan. Opened in that magical Chicago centenary year of 1933, it continues to be improved. Today LSD, as it is known in Chicago, is on many short lists of the most scenic road trips in the United States.

The Commission's plans were long delayed by the Great Depression, then WWII, but road traffic decreased in those two periods so the problems did not worsen for a time. With the return of prosperity in post-war America, the traffic problems returned and grew quickly. There were some early by-pass projects completed. The Kingery or "Tri-state (Illinois, Indiana & Wisconsin) Highway" was completed in 1950. The Edens Expressway in 1951. Neither of these even came close to being a crosstown route for they were built through farmlands and rural villages which would one day become crowded suburbs. Land was relatively cheap, not much court action was needed to take it, and few buildings had to be razed.

The construction of a cross-town expressway, on the other hand, meant building through long-existing neighborhoods from the Near West Side to Roosevelt Road. In order to do this, hundreds of buildings would need to be torn down in its path, hundreds of businesses displaced, and thousands of residents made homeless. Massive funding was necessary, but since there was nothing interstate about the new superhighway, federal motor-fuel taxes could not be tapped. The funds came from the city, Cook County, and the State of Illinois. Since all three were well controlled by the Democratic Party, the appropriation of tax money was easily obtained. In the end, the crosstown expressway cost $185,000,000, a lot of money in the 1950s but today an amount that might be spent on complex interchanges.

The hard part was going to be the dispossessing of those thousands of residents who loved their homes, apartments, and neighborhoods. The project was literally and figuratively "steamrolled" with the power of political clout, propaganda, and eminent domain. Eminent domain is the power of a government entity to "take" private property against the wishes of the property owner if it can be shown to be needed "for

Destruction during the building of the Eisenhower Expressway.

a greater good." Eminent domain is easier if it can be shown that the property being taken is not worth more money that the government's initial offer, let alone being protected. All the proponents of the new highway, city and county government, business entities, and even the press cooperated in an effort to discredit the neighborhoods.

It was true at the time that some of the city's worst housing and "skid rows" were on the Near West Side and some of the apartment buildings were substandard but that did not warrant the toxic campaign which generalized the neighborhoods as "slums" or "blighted." In one of its less glorious moments, the press saw this as a project that would kill two birds with one stone: build a needed superhighway and slum clearance at the same time. Here are the words of Mayor Martin Kennelly, "Just wiping out slums, that alone has made the work worthwhile. And we've gone far enough with the construction that any imagination can foresee the revitalization of the Near West Side which means so much to Chicago."

Those who lived in the path of destruction had few advocates. Since the scale of eminent domain was unprecedented and the residents felt there was no way to fight city hall, they were naive and unorganized. There were no grass-roots activists to organize opposition as would regularly occur from the '60s onward. They became victims of progress.

The concept of the crosstown superhighway had been talked about for so long without action and began so abruptly that most residents didn't understand the impact it would have on their lives until it was too late. Some had to be forcibly evicted. A few held out literally until the building next door was being torn down.

"Blighted" and "slum" are relative terms. Families living in the neighborhoods certainly did not consider it in that way. To them, neighborhood life was comfortable, convenient, and safe. For example, Jim O'Neill, who lived on Van Buren St. in the 1940s says, "I don't think our building was run-down." When he looked at old photographs he responds, "It certainly doesn't look like that to me. Little by little the buildings came down. I have vivid memories of these piles of rubble. My sister and I would go out and play in the rubble . . . There would be these piles of beams that would be burning." Surely he wasn't the only one who was reminded of photographs of bombed-out cities in Europe after WWII.

With so little time for planning, residents were confused about what to do next. The taking of property meant the landlords got the payments, such as they were. The tenants were left with no money and no home. To make matters worse, there was a lingering post-war housing shortage which drove prices up, adding expense to the confusion and heartbreak of leaving their friends, family, and neighbors for good. There was a half-hearted attempt to help resettle residents, but the need was so great and the taking so abrupt it was of little help. If these displaced persons moved to an established neighborhood within the city they would have to fit in at new schools, new churches, make new friends, learn new ways, find new routes to work, or new jobs altogether. The culmination of all of this while suddenly surrounded by strangers took a tremendous toll. They might well be seen as interlopers and ostracized.

The 1950s were a period of exponential growth of the suburbs fueled by the housing shortage and "White Flight" from racial tensions in the city. Those who could moved to suburbs to find members of their own ethnic group. Others would find adjusting to the suburbs easier because those living in these developments were all new residents, all strangers needing to find new connections. The same changes cannot be said for many minorities who would not be welcome in most neighborhoods. Consider these coded words from the *Chicago Tribune* in 1949, "Today the community population of 50,000 includes chiefly persons of Italian, Mexican, Greek, Jewish and Negro ancestry." Existing property covenants and "red-lining" (The unofficial lines realtors drew around certain neighborhoods to deny sales to minorities) were used to restrict where most could move. This was especially true of the expanding Black population. Poverty and hopelessness have grown along with high unemployment, drug dealing, and some of the worst gang violence in the city. If this is a sample of the expressed goal of "improving" the neighborhoods, it has been a criminal failure. Fortunately, there are better examples. The closer you get to downtown the more gentrification there has been so that safe and trendy, re-invented neighborhoods are thriving. Still, travelers on the expressway are warned that getting off at any street they do not know well can be dangerous.

As far back as the early 1930s, the course of the new expressway had been determined. When the new main Chicago post office opened in 1933 it had a six-lane-wide gap at the base for the future superhighway. Construction began in 1949. Instead of a steady progression westward from Downtown, the work was done on seven sections simultaneously to speed completion. The destruction and construction were the same in every section. Buildings in the path were razed and the rubble was burned or removed for lakefront fill. The highway route was dug down several feet below surface street level to allow arterial routes to cross it on bridges with a clearance of fourteen feet. The sunken roads' surface also allowed entrance and exit ramps with minimum need for taking more property.

The many, many streets which had no bridges just ended at one side of the expressway and resumed on the other side. You may as well have moved the divided sections of the neighborhoods to different parts of the city.

Neighborhoods were not the only thing split in two. Two cemeteries, Forest Home and Concordia were in the way. There was some early talk about elevating the new road over them but it died quickly when the added expense and time needed to build them was considered. Instead, the graves of 3,500 people were disinterested and the bodies moved to other cemeteries. Since these were largely neighborhood and family burial grounds of long standing it meant additional sadness for families. Now they had to travel farther to find the new graves or in some cases might never find the new site of burial.

The guiding principle of construction was to get as much done as fast and cheaply as possible. For want of a better term, the expressway design was "brutal." In that regard, no thought or funds were given over to softening the design with more pleasant landscaping. This was the pragmatic "City That Works" after all.

The first of the seven sections were opened to public use in 1955. It was not very convenient because it was unconnected to any other completed section. Sections had staggered openings until the last section opened in 1960. The expressway planners and promoters fully expected the newly named Congress St. Expressway to ease traffic coming into and out of the city for years. In this respect, they were all terribly short-sighted. Within months of its opening, it was choked with traffic. Confusing ramp locations and lane reductions made the problems worse. Accidents were soon being measured in the hundreds.

Probably the worst planned section of Congress St. was at its western terminus where it joined or attempted junctions with surface streets, toll roads, and interstates. It was a design so poorly thought out that it even got its own infamous nickname, "The Hillside Strangler" for the small city where it was located. The congestion has since been eased to a large degree by a massive multi-year reconstruction that caused traffic headaches of its own. It should be no surprise that the "improvement" cost more to build than the entire expressway cost.

Since its official opening in 1960, the Congress St. Expressway has had two name changes. When it connected to the Interstate Highway system on its western end it was designated I-290 which is how you'd find it on navigation systems. Later it was named to honor the godfather of the interstate system, President Dwight D. Eisenhower. Democratic Chicago and Cook County choose not to object to the name change.

One forward-thinking aspect planned was leaving a wide enough median on the Eisenhower as well as the Kennedy and the Dan Ryan (much more politically acceptable names) for rapid transit. It was thought completing the Blue Line as a combination subway, surface and elevated route from downtown to Oak Park would reduce vehicle traffic, but that did not happen. Before the westward shift of population, there was a definite and predictable rush hour into the city in the morning hours and out in the evenings. Long before the present, that separation blurred as a reverse commute took effect. As many people leave to work in the suburbs as drive from the suburbs to the city. Even traffic in the wee hours and on weekends is heavy as people came into the city for night-time dining and entertainment.

From its original construction to its present woes of unavoidable creeping, clogged traffic, and need for constant maintenance due to heavy use and Chicago winters, it's hard to find anything good to say about the Eisenhower. There are alternative routes on other expressways like the Stevenson or even on surface streets if you know the way, but they are often as slow. The best the Eisenhower's users will call it is a necessary evil and it is impossible for younger generations to imagine Chicago without it. Most commuters have come to have a grudging respect for the old devil and simply call it "The Ike." You'll excuse me if I observe that few, if any, will go as far as to say "I Like The Ike."

21

SPOOKY CHICAGO

GHOSTS, GRAVEYARDS, TRAGEDY, AND MURDER

If you are a stranger to Chicago or even a new resident and you want to explore the city but aren't sure where to begin, you might want to take a tour. There will be dozens to choose from including a neighborhood tour or tours of Wrigley and Guaranteed Rate Fields (or whatever the park where the White Sox play is currently named). If you like cuisine there are restaurant tours both trendy and ethnic. You could do a tour of landmarks such as the Willis and Tribune Towers and the Wrigley Building. If you fancy fine arts you won't find a better place to visit than the Chicago Institute of Art. Maybe a historic tour or two. Every kind of tour from architectural to the Lincoln Park Zoo. And this being Chicago, a gangster tour of course. Now, how do you want to get around? Self-guided and guided walking tours, narrated river boat cruises, bicycle tours, single and double level bus tours, even horse-drawn carriage and Segway tours are ready for you, take your pick.

If you'd like some thrills and chills on your tour you could do worse than find one of those which specialize in Haunted Chicago. After all, the city has a reputation as one of the most haunted metropolitan areas in America. Did you know that? If you're a believer in the occult world, so much the better, but even if you aren't, you'll learn about places where strange phenomena exist. Or do they? Naturally, or supernaturally if you prefer, you'll find a treasure trove of hauntings in this fair city. Restless souls everywhere seeking something we can only surmise.

Graveyards are a good place to start. Two of the best prospects are Graceland and Rosehill. Graceland, in the Uptown neighborhood practically in the shadow of Wrigley Field, is enthralling and not just because of spirits. Some of the city's and the nation's most influential people chose Graceland for its beauty and architecture. Graceland rightfully boasts an illustrious list of the rich and famous but that doesn't by itself explain the hauntings. You'll find a much better prospect when you come across the mass grave of dead from the terrible Iroquois Theater fire in 1903. Because Graceland was once far outside the city limits, hundreds of graves in the old city cemetery in what is now Lincoln Park were disturbed by disinterring the dead whom it was believed were the cause of typhoid fever, cholera, or malaria. Reburying them here may have agitated many old souls.

By far the most famous haunting may not be a burial at all. Within Graceland is an extraordinary marble sculpture of a young girl seated on a log chair dressed in Victorian fashion. Now protected by a glass case to keep it from dissolving in acid rain, it's said that sometimes a visitor will look at the case only to find the figure gone and at the same time notice a similar girl wandering nearby. But as the girl disappears, the sculpture reappears in the case. Spooky, right? Maybe, until you do some debunking research. The carving on the marker's pedestal reads "Inez Clark." Ghost hunters may not wish to know that a careful search of cemetery records shows that no one with that name is laid to rest at Graceland. In fact, the statue may be nothing more than a salesman's sample. It wasn't unusual in the old days for stone carvers to advertise themselves by putting an impressive example of their work in a busy section of the cemetery. The site of "Inez Clark" isn't in a busy place anymore but the marker remains.

Another Chicago cemetery which has a reputation for haunting is Rosehill. The body of fifteen-year-old Bobby Franks, the victim of Nathan Leopold and Dickie Loeb's cold-blooded "thrill killing," lays here. It is legend that his apparition wandered the grounds, but hasn't been seen since Leopold's death in 1971. There is another possibility that is less

Sculpture of Inez Clark located in Graceland Cemetery.

well known. The city wanted to buy the property from a farmer named Hiram Roe. Before he sold it, he insisted on keeping the original name of Roe's Hill. Sometime years ago, a clerical error caused a misspelling and conflated the two words to Rosehill. Maybe the disgruntled ghost of Farmer Roe is haunting the place.

There are dozens of haunted buildings as well, even, with apologies to Disney World, a Haunted Mansion. It was once the palatial residence of Marshall Field. His son and successor committed suicide there and reportedly the home soon became uninhabitable due to so many apparitions and constant unexplainable noises. Eventually the mansion was sold to a developer who has reconfigured it for luxury condominiums. Makes you wonder if the ghosts are gone or the new condo owners share the strange occurrences.

Surely your ghost tour would not be complete without a visit to the Biograph Theater on North Lincoln Avenue, the scene of the ambush set up by FBI Special Agent Melvin Purvis. Purvis had become obsessed with bringing justice to John Dillinger whom he hated for slipping away from six other chances of apprehension in which several people including policemen were killed, mostly by friendly fire.

A young woman who was a friend of Dillinger's Chicago girlfriend, Polly Hamilton, made a deal with the FBI. She called herself Anna Sage, but her real name was Ana Cupanus. Capunas was facing deportation action. She told Purvis that in exchange for the deportation proceedings being erased, she would set up Dillinger by wearing a bright red dress when the three went to a specific showing of the film *Manhattan Melodrama* at the Biograph. Ever since, she has been known as "The Lady in Red." When the film was done and Dillinger and the women left, Purvis approached and told Dillinger to surrender. Instead he ran into an alley and as he drew a gun was immediately shot multiple times by FBI agents. One of the bullets disfigured his face when it tore through his spine and brain, exiting just below his right eye. Dillinger died at the scene despite attempts to revive him.

Thus was the violent end of a violent life. Or was it? There are many who believe that it wasn't Dillinger who was killed but a minor hoodlum wannabe named Jimmy Lawrence. That Ana Sage had set up the wrong man and Purvis covered up the fact. Lawrence was said to resemble Dillinger's appearance and in fact, Dillinger had had recent facial surgery to change his looks. The dead man in the alley was supposed to be shorter and more muscular than Dillinger and Lawrence disappeared after the ambush. But, then again so did Dillinger. Did he give up his life of crime or was he mistakenly shot to death by federal agents? There is a version of the story that would have you believe that Jimmy Lawrence was the last alias used by Dillinger explaining the disappearance of both men. Whatever the truth, the alley near the Biograph is said to be haunted and an apparition of a man running down the alley, falling, and then disappearing has been reported.

Speaking of buildings and alleys, Chicago has a "Death Alley." It is at the scene of the terrible Iroquois Theater fire in 1903 which ended over six hundred lives. Rather than burn to death, dozens of people died as they jumped from a fire escape that had never been connected to the ground. The theater building is long gone, but the alley remains. Those brave enough to enter sometimes feel cold drafts and hear screams from invisible sources.

Be sure to include a visit the so-called most haunted building in Chicago, the Congress Park Hotel on Congress Street near the lakefront. Al Capone had a suite here that was his Chicago headquarters. How many gangland slayings do you thing were ordered from there? Several rooms in the Congress are so prone to paranormal activity that they have been abandoned and sealed shut, their doors hidden behind plaster and wallpaper. Footsteps in empty corridors have been reported and noises seem to come from the walls while others report that lights flicker from time-to-time. A Steven King short story, "Room 1408" is thought to be inspired by that room in the Congress Park which is never occupied by the living.

The Congress Park was much newer at the time of the World's Columbian Exhibition in 1892. Then, it was the place where America's first serial killer, H.H. Holmes, lured naive young women to his "hotel." H.H. Holmes' "hotel" quickly came to be called the "Murder Castle" when it was searched after Holmes' arrest. Inside was a warren of small rooms for torture and asphyxiation, a maze with no exit to frighten his victims, trapdoors, hidden staircases, and greased chutes to allow him to get bodies to the basement without having to carry them. In the basement was a large vat of acid and lye used to dissolve even the bones of his victims. All of this was the ingenious creation of a madman, of course. Later investigation showed that H.H. Holmes was only one of a half dozen or more names he used. After all, when your real name is Henry Webster Mudgett you might want to change it to ironically honor the most famous private detective of all time. Mudgett, or Holmes, if you prefer, confessed to the murder of more than two hundred people, but the evidence recovered showed the number to be nine, easily enough to cause him to be hanged in 1896. The Murder Castle is gone, its macabre reputation replaced by a post office.

Ft. Dearborn was part of the oldest section of Chicago. It was a hastily-built stockade which was designed as a shelter for nearby settlers who were still in the middle of Native American lands. During the War of 1812, the Pottawatomie Indians agreed to help the British rid the area of Americans whom they saw as a plague, claiming their lands and desecrating their culture. During one uprising, settlers fled to the fort for protection. Indeed the fort was soon surrounded by hostile Pottawatomie. The captain of the troops stationed there negotiated a bargain with the Pottawatomie chiefs. In return for safe passage, he would trade the guns, powder, and stores from the fort. When he returned and explained the agreement there was a mutiny of sorts when the military contingent refused to agree and to emphasize their disgust broke the muskets in pieces and threw them with the powder and gallons of whiskey down an abandoned well. In further talks Capt. Wells was again guaranteed safe passage by some chiefs but not all. Not long after a column of settlers and soldiers left the fort along the lake shore it was attacked by Pottawatomie hidden behind nearby dunes. The fight was so one-sided it was rightly called a massacre. Besides the soldiers who were killed, eighty-six adult and twelve child pioneers were victims.

The exact location of the Ft. Dearborn Massacre was soon lost. Decades later when the land was much more valuable and an area was being excavated for a new building, human remains were found which were originally thought to be a mass grave of one of the city's epidemics. When the bones were more accurately dated, it was shown that they had been there since early in the nineteenth century. The land along the Chicago River was too valuable not to build on so the site of the fort is gone. Since the skeletons have been exposed there have been reports of people dressed in pioneer clothes running and falling. A nearby plaque denotes the story of Ft. Dearborn. Bronze markers embedded in the sidewalk at the corner of Michigan Ave and E. Wacker Drive denote the shockingly small size of the structure.

Chicago has seen its share of tragic fires. Everyone knows about the Great Chicago Fire of 1871 and how it destroyed a huge swath of the city leaving the iconic water tower spared. Sometimes a ghostly figure is seen in one window or another. You have already read of the horrors of the Iroquois Theater fire. The Lady of the Angels school fire is not well known outside the city. On December 1st, 1958 a smoldering, smoky fire started in a basement trash can. When a door was opened, enough oxygen was sucked into the fire that it virtually exploded into a fireball which spread upwards. Most of the children and nuns were able to escape but many were trapped on the upper floors. The poisonous smoke killed many, as did the fire. A few were lucky enough to jump or climb to safety when firemen arrived. Safety came too late for ninety-four children and three nuns. Few hauntings have been reported there perhaps because the original building was torn down and maybe because all those lost souls were gathered in by the Lady of The Angels.

The worst disaster in Chicago's history is the sinking of the excursion boat SS *Eastland* in the Chicago River. Over 800 lives were lost, too many of them children. Twenty-one complete families perished in the sinking between the Clark and LaSalle Street bridges. All that remains now is another one of those ominous commemorative bronze plaques briefly telling of the tragedy. That, and the reports of passersby who experience apparitions and cold breezes on hot days.

In 1927, an event took place which established Chicago as the center of gangland violence. In a garage on Clark St., members of "Bugs" Moran's South Side gang were gathered on a February day. There was a knock on the door and several other hoodlums disguised in police uniforms entered with "Tommy" guns ready. The gangsters were lined up against a wall and mowed down in the legendary St. Valentine's Day Massacre. No one was ever brought to trial for the slayings, not surprising in a city controlled by several gangs, only one of which was loyal to

Al Capone. The building has since been torn down. There's nothing left now but a vacant lot because, so far, no one has attempted to build on it.

There are many more stops on the ideal ghost tour of the toddling town. In the city, you can find the site of the grisly Sausage Murder, the crimes of Richard Speck, the Haymarket Square Riot, and if a place should ever be haunted, it is the site of the Union's version of Andersonville prison during the Civil War. Thousands of Confederate soldiers died from exposure, malnutrition, and disease in what came to be called "Eighty Acres of Hell." Don't neglect the site of the tragic crash of Flight 191 near O'Hare Airport or even The House of Weird Death. Yes, that's what it was called.

If you want to go beyond the city limits, you'll find more haunting. You'll find where Leopold and Loeb murdered Bobby Franks and the tragic sites of John Wayne Gacy's murders. There are the places where more children have been murdered. Barbara and Patricia Grimes, a crime which has never been solved and those of Anton and John Schuessler and Bobby Peterson, which was solved after decades of being a cold case. The places still haunt. You can visit the places where the Chicago area's most famous hitchhiking ghost, Resurrection Mary, has been seen numerous times and even given rides. Visit Mt. Carmel, Archer Woods, St James Sag Church and Cemeteries, and Robinson Woods, a haunted ancient Indian burial mound. Woodlawn Cemetery in Forest Park is the site of "Showman's Rest," the mass burial of fifty-three mostly unnamed victims of a tragic 1918 circus train wreck in Hammond, Indiana. In Cicero is the Lexington Hotel, Al Capone's haven in that mob-controlled town, and not too long ago the site of Geraldo Rivera's anti-climactic opening of those mysterious empty hidden vaults.

SELECTED BIBLIOGRAPHY

Branigan, Michael. *A History of Chicago's O'Hare Airport*. Charleston: The History Press, 2011.

Haugh, Dolores. *Images of America: Riverview Amusement Park*. Chicago: Arcadia Publishing, 2004.

Johnson, James J. *A Century of Chicago Streetcars 1858–1958*. Wheaton, IL: The Traction Orange Company, 1964.

Samors, Neal, and Christopher Lynch. *Now Arriving: Traveling to and From Chicago By Air, 90 Years of Flight*. Chicago: Chicago Books Press, 2015.

ACKNOWLEDGMENTS

As I mentioned in the forward, my book would not have been written without the patient and endless help of my wife, Sue. I also owe a debt of gratitude to my faithful proofreader and friend, Eloise LaPalio. She also helped me with details about Chicago since she, and not I, grew up there. I also received a bit of a revelation from the author of *Love and Other Consolation Prizes*, Jamie Ford. In his book he mentioned a couple of midway rides and an exhibit at the 1909 Seattle World's Fair which were subsequently purchased and transported to Riverview Park. The excellent photos of the WWII aircraft at both Midway and O'Hare Airports were printed with permission from Travel for Aircraft. Also, I definitely need to give credit to my editor, Erika Hodges, for her many hours of review and good suggestions. I am also grateful to my formatting editor Crystal Devine whose wizardry in finding illustrations more than made up for my lack of skill in finding them on the internet.

The photo credit for the author photo belongs to Carolyn O'Leary.

ABOUT THE AUTHOR

JAMES DOHREN is a long-retired middle school social studies teacher. He and his wife, Susan, spend half of each year in Florida and the other half in Pennsylvania. They have a daughter in each state so they are always near family. James is the author of *Letters from a Shoebox*, transcriptions and commentary on seventeen Civil War letters also published by Sunbury Press.